Cognitive Processes

INTRODUCTORY PSYCHOLOGY

This series of titles is aimed at psychology students in sixth forms and further education colleges and at those wishing to obtain an overview of psychology. The books are easy to use, with comprehensive notes written in coherent language; clear flagging of key concepts; relevant and interesting illustrations; well-defined objectives and further reading sections to each chapter; and self-assessment questions at regular intervals throughout the text.

Published

INDIVIDUAL DIFFERENCES   Ann Birch and Sheila Hayward

DEVELOPMENTAL PSYCHOLOGY   Ann Birch and Tony Malim

COGNITIVE PROCESSES   Tony Malim

SOCIAL PSYCHOLOGY   Tony Malim and Ann Birch

COMPARATIVE PSYCHOLOGY   Tony Malim, Ann Birch and Sheila Hayward

PERSPECTIVES IN PSYCHOLOGY   Tony Malim, Ann Birch and Alison Wadeley

Forthcoming

BIOPSYCHOLOGY   Sheila Hayward

RESEARCH AND STATISTICAL METHODS   Tony Malim and Ann Birch

Series Standing Order

If you would like to receive future titles in this series as they are published, you can make use of our standing order facility. To place a standing order please contact your bookseller or, in case of difficulty,write to us at the address below with your name and address and the name of the series. Please state with which title you wish to begin your standing order. (If you live outside the United Kingdom we may not have the rights for your area, in which case we will forward your order to the publisher concerned.)

Customer Services Department, Macmillan Distribution Ltd
Houndmills, Basingstoke, Hampshire RG21 6XS, England

COGNITIVE PROCESSES

Attention, Perception, Memory, Thinking and Language

Tony Malim

MACMILLAN

First published 1994 by
THE MACMILLAN PRESS LTD
Houndmills, Basingstoke, Hampshire RG21 2XS
and London
Companies and representatives
throughout the world

ISBN 0–333–58811–8

A catalogue record for this book is available
from the British Library.

10   9   8   7   6   5   4   3
03   02   01   00   99   98   97   96

Printed in Malaysia

Cartoons by Sally Artz

Contents

List of Figures

Preface

The aim of this book is to provide an introduction to some of the ways in which psychologists have investigated cognition, and to examine critically some of their more significant findings. The focus is upon cognitive processes, which include attention, perception, memory thinking and language. Chapter 1 provides a brief introduction to cognitive processes and examines some of the methods researchers have used in this area. Chapters 2 to 5 look in turn at attention, perception, memory and finally thinking and language.

As with the rest of the books in this series the intention is to provide a concise framework of comprehensive notes, which may either be used as a basis for further study or for revision purposes. Each chapter begins with objectives to be met and at the end of each section there are self-assessment questions to help independent students test their understanding of the section. Readers are advised to work carefully through the text one section at a time before considering the self assessment questions following it. After further study or reading the questions may be re-examined.

The prime focus of the book is upon GCE A-level and GCSE. It should, however, prove useful to anyone encountering psychology for the first time. This might include students on degree courses, student nurses or midwives, BTEC students and those on teaching courses. I have every confidence that this book will prove to be as useful and popular as the previous titles in this series and above all I hope you will find it enjoyable.

Tony Malim

Acknowledgements

The author and publishers are grateful to the following for permission to reproduce illustrations:

Figure 3.12 reprinted with permission from *Understanding Psychology* by C. B. Dobson, M. Hardy, S. Heyes, A. Humphreys and P. Humphreys, published by Weidenfeld & Nicolson.

Figure 3.19 reprinted with permission from *Art and Illusion* by E. H. Gombrich, published by Phaidon Press.

Figure 3.22 reprinted with permission from *Child Development: a first course* by Kathy Sylva and Ingrid Lunt, published by Basil Blackwell.

Figure 3.23 reprinted with permission from *Understanding Children's Development* by Peter Smith and Helen Cowie, published by Basil Blackwell.

Figure 3.24 reprinted by permission from page 123 of *Psychology* (2nd edition) by John Dworetsky, copyright © 1985 by West Publishing Company. All rights reserved.

Thanks are due also to Sally Artz who is responsible for the cartoons at the beginning of each chapter.

Introduction to Cognitive Processes 1

At the end of this chapter you should be able to:

1. Describe the cognitive approach to psychology.
2. Identify the distinction between 'top down' and 'bottom up' approaches.
3. Distinguish between parallel processing and serial processing.
4. Identify some of the methods used to explain cognitive processes.

What are Cognitive Processes?

Human beings (in common with other animals) function at various levels. At the most basic level, systems exist within the brain to control physiological functioning. The monitoring of bodily needs, such as the need for food and drink, for fresh air and sleep is part of the function of the lower brain. Cognitive processes on the other hand relate to those functions which have their control within the higher brain centres of the cortex. To an extent it is the development of a more complex cortical function to override and complement the lower brain which distinguishes human beings from animals. Cognition tends to be concerned with conscious rather than unconscious processes, though there is some overlap, and with voluntary rather than involuntary responses. The particular areas of cognition dealt with in this book include selective attention, perception, memory, language and thought.

Historical Background

It is important to understand the historical background to the present study of cognition. Hearnshaw (1987) claims that cognitive psychology is both one of the oldest and also one of the newest parts of psychology.

1

Wundt and Introspection

In 1879 William Wundt opened the first psychological laboratory in Leipzig. His proposition was that students of psychology should study conscious experience. The method chosen was introspection. Trained observers paid careful attention to their sensations and reported them as objectively as possible when they were presented with stimuli. Wundt's programme was maintained continuously for the next 50 years. Emphasis was placed on the careful training of observers, control of their observations and on replication (that is, repetition of experiments).

Ebbinghaus, too, whose work is described in more detail in Chapter 4 contributed to the early study of cognition. He tested his own ability to memorise nonsense syllables under a wide variety of circumstances. Nonsense syllables were used in an attempt to ensure that all the material to be remembered was equally lacking in meaning. It was apparent that differences in meaningfulness influenced the ease (or difficulty) which individuals experienced in recall.

William James, however, preferred a less formal approach to the study of the human mind, and of memory in particular. He was more concerned with problems which occurred in daily life than with the memorisation of nonsense syllables. He drew a distinction between memory process and memory structure. His proposal that there were two different kinds of memory foreshadowed the model-building of much of the later research.

Behaviourism

The behaviourists, led by Watson and Thorndike, suggested that introspection was unscientific. Consciousness was far too vague to be studied scientifically. The emphasis moved to 'observable behaviour'. For instance, with regard to the fairly central issue of learning, this was seen to be a matter of changes in observable behaviour rather than of something which happened in the mind. So Thorndike (1898) experimented with cats in puzzle boxes (crates hammered together from wooden slats, about 50 cm square and 30 cm high). The cats were hungry and there was a piece of fish clearly visible outside the box. An arrangement of strings, pulleys and catches allowed the door to be opened: the cats scrabbled and scratched until by chance they triggered the release mechanism to open the door. On average this took five minutes or so of random scratching to begin with, but after ten or twenty trials they would escape within five seconds. This demonstrated **trial and error learning**. He and other behaviourists, such as Watson and later Skinner were interested in the association between stimulus input (the situation the cat found itself in) and the response output (the scrabbling and the escape from the box).

The contributions made by behaviourists include:

- *Careful definition of concepts.* They were very careful to define the concepts with which they were dealing. Trial and error learning was very carefully differentiated from insightful learning (an example of which is Köhler's account of the chimpanzee Sultan described on page 139).
- *Experimental control of variables.* There was great attention paid to careful experimental control. Even with Thorndike's rather rudimentary experiments there was great care taken to control the variables involved (the detail of the release mechanism, the hunger of the animals and the food presented outside the cage). Skinner's later experiments with rats in 'Skinner boxes' were elaborately and scientifically controlled. Schedules of reinforcement were devised which carefully controlled the way in which pellets of food were given to the animals as reinforcement (or reward) for pressing a lever within the box.

Gestalt Psychology

The emphasis of the Gestalt psychologists was on humans' innate capacity to organise the material they encountered so that it became meaningful. A tune, for example, is more than simply the sum of its musical notes. Its Gestalt is the pattern of sound which it creates as a whole. They objected to the analysis of experience into its separate components because they felt that the whole was greater than the sum of its parts. They also stressed the importance of **insight**, the way in which the various parts of a problem, which seem at first unrelated to each other, may come together in a flash to form a coherent pattern. There is further discussion of this in

Chapter 3 (pp. 55–6) in relation to perception and in Chapter 5 (pp. 139–40) in relation to thinking.

Emergence of Cognitive Psychology

The factors which contributed to the emergence of cognitive psychology in the late 1950s and the early 1960s seem to have included the following:

1. The behaviourist approach, especially in the USA, seemed to be inadequate to explain complex human behaviour. Behaviourist learning theory, an approach based upon stimulus/response and reinforcement, was increasingly falling short of providing satisfactory explanations.
2. Chomsky, researching language acquisition, rejected behaviourist explanations of it. The structure of language was too complex to be explained in behaviourist terms. His contention that humans have an inborn capacity to master language conflicted with behaviourists' belief in a 'tabula rasa' (the notion put forward originally by John Locke in the 18th century that the human mind was a **blank sheet** at birth and that all human behaviour was learned).
3. Piaget's constructivist approach to child development, which concentrated on the establishment of concepts, was causing something of a revolution in primary education in the 1950s and 1960s. It suggested that what he termed **schemata** were established, as children developed, as a result of what they experienced. These schemata represented the basic building blocks of intelligence. A fuller account of Piaget's research can be found in Birch and Malim (1988, Chapter 3).
4. The advent of computers encouraged an information processing approach in the communication and computer sciences which appealed to some psychologists.
5. The needs of military technology were also providing a spur for development in this area. Much of the work done on attention and vigilance, described in Chapter 2, was the result of operational needs arising during the Second World War. For instance, Mackworth's researches into sustained attention (pp. 27–8) resulted from the need for radar operators and others to maintain their vigilance over long periods.

Some Methods used by Cognitive Psychologists

Modelling

It is common for cognitive psychologists to attempt to build up a **model** of how the brain might be operating in a particular set of circumstances. This is an elaborate hypothesis which is open to testing by means of experiment. An example of this is the template-matching model to explain pattern recognition. This model hypothesises that when we see a face, in order to be able to recognise it we must mentally match it against the 'templates' of all the faces stored in our memory until we come upon one which fits perfectly. The model describes a theoretical process which might be going on in the brain and which can be tested experimentally. In this case the model turned out not to be a very satisfactory one, as will be explained in Chapter 3.

Advantages and Limitations of Modelling

On the positive side, modelling allowed researchers to come to grips in a meaningful way with the processes within the brain. Instead of saying, as behaviourists had done, that these were inaccessible to research they could make an informed guess about what was happening in the brain which could be verified (or discounted) by empirical research. On the minus side, it made great demands upon the creativity of researchers. The hypotheses to be tested resulted from speculation about what might be happening. If they were wildly adrift, much time and resources could be lost. However, if the informed guesswork was accurate, important insights might be gained.

Information Processing

This is an approach to the study of cognitive processes which has become increasingly popular among psychologists. It has two important components:

1. Mental processes are seen as a flow of information through various stages, which can be represented on a flow-chart. This includes both the flow of information within a person's mind,

and also the flow of information between the individual and the environment.
2. Mental processes may be better understood by comparing them with the operation of a computer with its three components: data, memory, and program.

The information processing approach 'can be seen as an attempt to understand the software of a very complex computer' (Evans, 1983). An example might make this clearer.

Suppose you want to post a letter. There could be several distinct stages in the operation:

1. Verify that the letter is ready to go (the address and the stamp are correct).
2. Find your way to the post box.
3. Ascertain that the post box is ready to receive the letter (i.e. that there will shortly be a collection).
4. Post the letter.

At each stage there there will be collection of data from the environment, more data recovered from memory and a program (a set of instructions). For instance, in relation to Stage 1. the visual sense provides information relating to the address and the stamp, and possibly further data from the address book, the memory supplies information about the correctness of the address and the right stamp to use and the program amounts to a set of steps to verify whether the letter is ready to go. The other stages can be broken down in the same way.

The advantages and disadvantages of an information processing approach include:

1. Each stage can be manipulated experimentally and observations made, especially of times taken for the stage.
2. A disadvantage is you are looking at each little bit of the process on its own without much reference either to the rest of the process or to the individual participant. There are also severe limitations to the computer analogy which will be discussed further in Chapter 5 of this book.

Ecologically Valid Methods

The results obtained in research need to hold good also 'in the real world'. Much research into memory, for instance, has been laboratory based and involved participants in memorising unrelated words or nonsense syllables. This is not the kind of task we engage in in everyday life! By contrast, Bartlett in his research described in Chapter 4 (pp. 91–3) focused upon meaningful material and natural situations. Ecologically valid research attempts to mirror more accurately what happens outside the laboratory. This includes material used (Bartlett's story to be recalled is closer to reality than Ebbinghaus's nonsense syllables), the participants employed and the context. Research into eyewitness testimony, absent-mindedness or the ability of teachers to remember the names and faces of the members of their classes is likely to be more ecologically valid than laboratory research into recall of isolated words. However, it is not so easy to obtain good control of variables in this kind of research. Perhaps the way forward is a combination of ecologically valid and laboratory based research. Attempts have been made in this book to examine both.

Cognitive Science

It is worthwhile to make a very brief mention of **cognitive science**, a developing discipline which relates to cognitive processing. At the present time Brown (1990) has suggested that this seems to take one of three forms:

1. As a completely new discipline with its own subject matter (intelligent systems, both natural and artificial), its own methods and its own vocabulary. It suggests that mental states can be replicated and studied by using computers.

2. As an umbrella discipline, providing a whole range of new tools for studying cognitive processes. These include:
    (a) The study of artificial intelligence, a branch of computer science which attempts to program computers to perform the kind of functions traditionally only associated with humans (language, for instance, or problem solving).

(b) Neuroscience, which relates to attempts to find neurological explanations for mental processes. Examples might be the experiments of Hubel and Wiesel (1962) who used micro-electrodes to pick up impulses from the visual cortex of a cat and found that particular cells in the visual cortex responded to lines of specific orientations (see Chapter 3 for further details), or the study of evoked cortical potentials, electrical signals generated by neurons just below an electrode placed on the scalp. This is mentioned further in Chapter 2.

3. As eco-cognitivism, a view which rejects the notion that it is possible to study mental states independently of the ecology in which they occur: that is to say, their causes and effects in the real world.

It is worthwhile mentioning in this introductory chapter some concepts which will crop up later in the book. These include distinctions made between **top-down** and **bottom-up** approaches and between **serial** and **parallel** processing.

Top-Down or Bottom-Up Processing

Top-down cognitive processing starts with the broad context within which processing occurs, that is, the needs of the individual and the setting, and only after that considers the detailed characteristics of the stimulus being processed. For instance, a top-down approach to how children learn to read suggests that they first make predictions about what the text is most likely to mean from contextual and other clues. The hypotheses formed are then tested against the available evidence, which includes context as well as the words and finally letters making up the words on the page. Bottom-up processing starts with the stimuli and only after they have been processed do other factors come into play. To take the same reading example, in a bottom-up model of reading a child starts with letters and the sounds they represent, then words, their sound and their meaning and only after this the context and the sense of the whole.

Serial or Parallel Processing

In serial processing the assumption is made that each stage of the processing sequence must be completed before the next is begun. Parallel processing on the other hand implies that more than one stage of processing may occur at any one time. For example, Allport and his colleagues suggested that it might be possible to pay attention to more than one thing at a time, provided that different senses were involved (Allport *et al.*, 1972). This would involve parallel processing. Broadbent on the other hand suggested that there was a single channel processing mechanism with one item being attended to at a time. This is serial processing. Both Allport's and Broadbent's models are discussed in Chapter 2 of this book.

Self-assessment Questions

1. What are some of the pre-cursors of modern cognitive psychology? What contributions have they made to its development?
2. What is meant by an 'information processing' approach to cognitive processes? What are some of the advantages and disadvantages of this approach?
3. Distinguish between:
   (a) serial and parallel processing;
   (b) top-down and bottom-up processing.

FURTHER READING

M. W. Eysenck *A Handbook of Cognitive Psychology* (Hillsdale, N.J.: Lawrence Erlbaum, 1984).
M. W. Matlin, *Cognition*, 2nd edition (Fort Worth: Holt, Rinehart & Winston, 1989).

Attentional Processes 2

At the end of this chapter you should be able to:

1. Describe what is meant by 'selective attention'.
2. Identify the problem of the 'cocktail party' phenomenon which Cherry investigated, and outline his conclusions.
3. Show an understanding of the theories and models of selective attention formulated by Broadbent, Treisman, Deutsch and Deutsch, and Kahneman.
4. Distinguish between unconscious and conscious attentional processes.
5. Describe some of the factors which influence divided attention.
6. Describe some of the research into sustained attention (or vigilance) and account for some of the findings.

SECTION I SELECTIVE ATTENTION

Human beings are constantly bombarded by stimuli from the world in which they live, but can only take in and use a very small portion of this material. There exist, therefore, mechanisms which enable them to select and process stimuli which are valuable, or of interest and to allow the rest to pass them by. This section will examine this process of **selective attention**.

To illustrate the way in which our attention is arrested and held, let us look at how advertisers attempt to attract our attention. Some of the characteristics of a stimulus which determine whether or not we will pay attention to it are the following:

1. Its intensity: a bright colour will attract us more than a dull one.
2. Its size: a large thing is more likely to seize our attention than something small.

3. Its duration or repetition: a fleeting stimulus will not catch our attention as easily as one which persists or is repeated.
4. Its emotional content: a stimulus which carries emotional overtones for us will attract us more than a neutral one.
5. Its suddenness or novelty: a sudden or unexpected stimulus is likely to catch our attention more easily than one we have been expecting or that we have encountered before.
6. Contrasting stimuli will attract attention more readily than those which are similar to each other.
7. Something which moves is more likely to attract attention than something stationary. When a rabbit is in danger from a predator it freezes, thus avoiding attracting the predator's attention.

Exercise

Watch a selection of advertisements on the commercial channels of television and write down briefly how the products being advertised are presented.

Experimental Studies of Attention

An early study relating to selective attention was that of Cherry (1953). His aims were:

1. To examine how individuals can focus on one conversation amid a babble of noise (as in a party).
2. To ascertain how much of the unattended material is retained.

In his experiments, participants had two messages presented to them, one to each ear. They were asked to **shadow** (listen particularly to and repeat out loud) one of them. They were then questioned to find out how much of each message they had retained. Of the unshadowed message physical characteristics only were extracted, for instance:

1. whether the voice was male or female;
2. how loud or soft it was; and
3. if a tone replaced speech.

Regarding content, very little was picked up. Subjects did not even notice if the speaker was using a foreign language, or if the speech was reversed. Processing of the unshadowed message seemed to be minimal.

Broadbent's Model of Selective Attention

Broadbent (1958) developed a model of selective attention as a result of his **split-span** experiments. These were experiments with **dichotic listening** (that is, listening to messages presented separately to each ear). For example, three pairs of digits were presented to each participant dichotically – three to one ear, three to the other – thus:

left	*right*
7	6
4	8
8	9

Participants found it much easier to recall all the digits from one ear then all from the other, rather than in pairs, as they had been presented: 748 then 689 rather than 76, 48, 89. When they were asked specifically to recall them in pairs they only managed 20 per cent correct recall.

Broadbent's explanation for this was that there is what he called a **sensory buffer** or filter. When two messages reach this filter together, one only can be processed; the other is reserved in the filter for future processing. The brain's limited processing capacity is thus not overloaded. Processing preference is determined by some physical attribute of the messages, in this case which ear received them first. Thus, the message to the right ear is reserved until all the left ear's message has been processed. Figure 2.1 illustrates Broadbent's model (Broadbent 1958). Other factors such as pitch or tone also seem to determine priority.

Broadbent envisages information from the senses being held briefly in a short-term memory store before passing to a **selective**

FIGURE 2.1

Broadbent's Model of Selective Attention

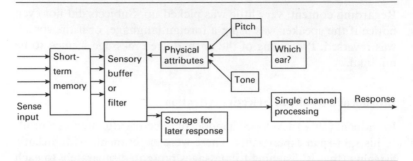

filter. This filter selects information on a physical basis, a high voice as opposed to a low voice or input from one ear as opposed to another. The selected information passes to a single channel processor and from there to the output stage, whatever response is required. Unselected information is retained for future processing.

While Broadbent's model dealt well with the phemonena which Cherry found in his shadowing trials, it had the limitation that it did not explain the 'cocktail party phenomenon'. An individual who has focused attention upon one conversation can nevertheless pick up relevant information from somewhere else in the room (a name for instance). This would indicate more than one level of selection. Moray (1959) tested this phenomenon by presenting a participant's name to the unattended ear while the participant was shadowing another message with the other ear. In nearly every case the name was picked up.

Other factors influencing processing include the following.

1. Experience of the participants

Underwood (1974) conducted similar experiments with participants who had had no experience of such tasks before, and compared their recall of pairs of digits with that of Moray, a researcher of great experience. While the naive participants could only manage 8 per cent recall, Moray managed 67 per cent.

2. The nature of the material

Allport *et al.* (1972) presented participants with different shadowing tasks. Passages from George Orwell's *Selected Essays* were presented to one ear to be shadowed, random words to be learned to the other. As might have been expected from Broadbent's model, very few words were recalled. However, when Allport replaced the words with a pictorial learning task, recall of the pictorial material was much better, suggesting that the dissimilarity of the two inputs was an important factor.

In an extension to this study Allport and his colleagues turned their attention to another kind of material, music. Participants were all skilled piano players. They had again to shadow continuous speech, but in this case they had at the same time to sight-read piano music from a score. As with the first experiment, the second task did not interfere. They were equally good at sight-reading with or without the shadowing task. The sight-reading task also seemed to have no effect on the accuracy with which they performed the shadowing task.

Shaffer (1975) in two experiments extended Allport's findings. In the first, a copy typist was made to shadow a piece of prose, heard over headphones while copy-typing a piece in German (a language she did not understand) from a visual presentation. In the second, the typist performed an audio-typing task, listening over headphones to material to be typed. She had at the same time one of two other tasks to perform: (a) She had to shadow a prose passage presented to the other ear; and (b) to read aloud a passage presented to her visually.

While the results in the first of these experiments showed little deterioration on the shadowing task, in the second there seemed to be considerable interference. These studies seem to lend some support to the view that separate channels are used to process different kinds of information.

3. Conscious or unconscious processing

Von Wright *et al.* (1975) suggested that failure to recall material presented to the unshadowed ear did not mean that it remained unprocessed. It may have been processed without conscious awareness. Their experiment was in two stages:

1. A long list of words was presented to participants. When the Finnish word for 'suitable' was presented they sometimes received an electric shock.
2. In the second stage of the experiment, participants shadowed one list of words while a second list presented to the other ear went unshadowed. In the unshadowed list was the previously shocked word, its synonym or its homonym (a word which either meant or sounded the same). When it was presented there was a noticeable change in galvanic skin response (GSR) (a measure of emotion). There had apparently been an emotional response to a word which had not been processed.

4. Meaning as a factor in selective attention

Gray and Wedderburn (1960) attempted to show that the meaning of messages to each ear had a bearing on which was selected. In a dichotic listening experiment participants were presented with digits interspersed with a coherent message. For example:

left ear	right ear
who	6
8	goes
there	7

Unlike participants in Broadbent's study, those in Gray and Wedderburn's experiment found little difficulty in recalling a coherent message 'Who goes there!' and then 687, even though the message had been presented partly to one ear, partly to the other.

Treisman's Attenuation Model

Treisman (1960, 1964a and b) used the shadowing technique originally developed by Cherry (p. 12). Participants had to repeat the message coming into one ear, the shadowed message, while ignoring the other, the unattended message. In one experiment, the shadowed message was in English, the unattended message was a French translation of it. The majority of participants recognised the meaning of the two messages as being the same, which supports

Gray and Wedderburn's finding that meaning is important in the selection process. There must have been some processing of the unattended message for its meaning to be appreciated. In a second experiment, both the shadowed and the unattended messages were slightly jumbled English sentences like 'I saw the girl song was wishing' and 'me that bird jumping in the street'.

When the first of the sentences was presented to the shadowed ear and the second to the unshadowed ear, participants tended to produce a verbal response something like:

'I saw the girl jumping, wishing . . . '

The word 'jumping' had intruded into the shadowed message in order to make more coherent sense of it. Where the shadowed sentence was already coherent sense, the intrusion did not occur.

In a further experiment, participants had to shadow a piece of normal prose, while the unattended ear received a string of words which only roughly resembled the structure of an English sentence. When the coherent message was switched without warning from the shadowed to the unattended ear, the response from the participants was to switch to shadowing the other ear. They were sometimes unaware that they had done this.

All these experiments provide evidence that there is at least some processing of the unselected messages.

The result of these experiments was a revision of Broadbent's model of selective attention to what became known as the **attenuation model**. While one channel is still selected on the basis of its physical properties, the filter does not completely block the unselected messages but weakens them, so that a stimulus of higher intensity is needed for them to be processed. Instead of the all-or-nothing processing which Broadbent's model implies, there is a focus on one input, while the others are weakened or attenuated. This attenuation model is illustrated in Figure 2.2.

You will see that besides the selected message there is also semantic processing of unselected material on the basis of what Treisman describes as a **dictionary unit**. This lists words and meanings each of which has a threshold (a minimum intensity at which that word will be recognised and used). The threshold will vary both in accordance with the importance an individual attaches to that word and also with expectations. The intruded word

FIGURE 2.2

Treisman's Attenuation Model of Selective Attention

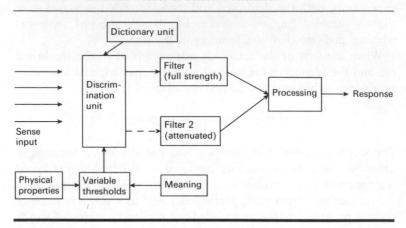

'jumping' in her experiment could be processed because the listener expected it to be used rather than the words received in the shadowed ear. It thus had a lower threshold than other words received by the unattended ear.

Treisman's model clearly resolves some of the difficulties with Broadbent's model, for example:

1. The processing according to meaning found by Gray and Wedderburn (p. 16).
2. It also provides an explanation for the 'cocktail party phenomenon', investigated by Cherry (p. 12).

But there remain two difficulties:

1. It is not clear what attenuation means. It is not that the stimulus becomes quieter, but that the information provided by the attenuated message is somehow reduced. It is hard to see how this works.
2. Recognising the meaning of a word or a passage requires extensive processing. The semantic analysis of the unattended

messages would need to be nearly as complete a process as the full processing of the attended message.

Pertinence (or Late Filter) Model of Selective Attention

Deutsch and Deutsch (1963) proposed a **pertinence** model of selective attention which placed the filter much closer to the output end of the processing system. This was subsequently revised by Norman (1968, 1969, 1976) and essentially proposes that all information is initially analysed for its pertinence, or relevance, and is then passed on to a filter if found to be pertinent (see Figure 2.3).

Evaluation of the Pertinence Model

There appear to be the following problems with this model:

1. Eysenck (1984) maintains this is a very uneconomical use of resources. It involves processing a large amount of material which is not going to be used.
2. Treisman and Geffen (1967) tested the model empirically. Participants in their study engaged in a shadowing task. They had to repeat the shadowed message aloud and also to indicate by tapping when they heard a certain target word (which might come into either ear). Deutsch and Deutsch's model would

---

FIGURE 2.3

Late Filter or Pertinence Model of Selective Attention (Deutsch and Deutsch and Norman)

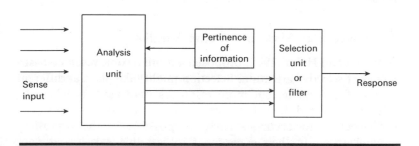

predict that the target word would be detected and would produce a response whichever ear it was presented to. The 'target' was, after all, pertinent. Treisman's (or Broadbent's) early filter model would predict that it would not be detected when it was presented to the unshadowed ear. Results supported Treisman – 87 per cent of the target words were detected in the shadowed, only 8 per cent in the unshadowed ear.

Deutsch and Norman (1967) rejected this as invalid. When the target was in the shadowed ear, participants had to shadow as well as tap; when it was in the other, they only had to tap. Treisman and Riley (1969) corrected this bias by telling participants to stop shadowing and tap as soon as they heard the target in either ear. There was still greater detection of shadowed than non-shadowed target words.

Limits to Processing Capacity

Broadbent, Treisman and Deutsch and Deutsch were all working on the basis that there was a limit to the processing capacity of the brain. Neisser (1976) disputed that such a limit existed:

> there is no physiologically or mathematically established limit on how much information we can pick up at once (Neisser, 1976 p. 96).

This limited capacity is not appropriate for an active developing structure such as the human brain. The brain contains millions of neurons (or nerve cells) which actively form interconnections with each other as stimuli from the environment reach it. While we may become inefficient when we try to do two things at once this becomes less so with practice.

A Resource-based Model of Selective Attention

Johnston and Heinz (1978) proposed a more flexible **resource-based** model of selective attention. Selection might take place at different stages of processing, but more resources were used up when the selection occurred closer to the response. There was thus a tendency for selection to occur as early as possible in the prevailing circumstances. In their experiment to test this, target and non-target words were presented simultaneously to both ears of participants. Target words were 'shadowed'. There were two conditions: (a) a low-sensory discrimination condition, where all the words were spoken by the same male voice; and (b) a high sensory-discrimination condition in which target words were spoken by a male voice, non-targets by a female voice.

The question at issue was this. In condition (b) it was possible to use sensory information based upon the voices used. In condition (a) only semantic information was available. There would be more complete processing of the non-target words, but more resources would be used. If Deutsch and Deutsch were right, there would be complete analysis under both conditions. Participants were found to be more able to recall non-target words in the low discrimination condition (a). This suggests that an early filter model such as Treisman's was more likely to be correct than Deutsch and Deutsch's late filter model.

Johnston and Wilson (1980) provided further backing for this. Participants had pairs of words which had at least two distinct meanings presented to them, one to each ear. For example, 'bears' might be a target word under the category 'wild animals'. Each target was accompanied by a word which qualified it appropriately (say, 'brown') or inappropriately (say, 'suffers') or else by a neutral control word such as 'vehicle'. There were two conditions: (a) a divided attention condition, in which the participant did not know which ear the target word was to be presented to; and (b) a focused attention condition in which participants were told to which ear the target word was to be presented.

In the 'divided attention' condition (a) it was found that detection of targets was easier with an appropriate accompanying word – 'brown' with 'bears' – than with a neutral word, and even more difficult with an inappropriate word.

In the 'focused condition' (b), the type of non-target word made no difference to the rate of detection. Processing seemed in this case to be carried out according to the physical factor, the ear to which the target was presented. In the 'divided condition' (a) semantic processing had to occur.

Self-assessment Questions

1. What were Cherry's findings in relation to the 'cocktail party phenomenon'?

2. What did Treisman's model of selective attention succeed in explaining, which Broadbent had not?
3. Describe the features of Deutsch and Deutsch's 'pertinence' model of selective attention.
4. In what way were Johnson and Heinz's conclusions a compromise between Treisman and Deutsch and Deutsch?

SECTION II   UNCONSCIOUS OR CONSCIOUS ATTENTIONAL PROCESSING

Schneider and Shiffrin (1977) distinguished between **controlled** and **automatic** processing. Controlled processing is serial (one thing is processed after another), automatic processing is parallel (more than one processing operation can occur at any one time). Difficult and unfamiliar tasks require controlled processing, simple and familiar tasks can be processed automatically. Participants in Schneider and Shiffrin's experiments saw a rapid sequence of 20 pictures in each trial.

In each picture (or frame) were four locations (see Figure 2.4), which could be occupied by a letter or by some dots. Participants had to look for and remember target letters in these frames.

Schneider and Shiffrin aimed to vary the difficulty of the task in various ways, through the number of the targets, the exposure time

---

FIGURE 2.4

Example of a Frame Similar to those in Schneider and Shiffrin's Experiments

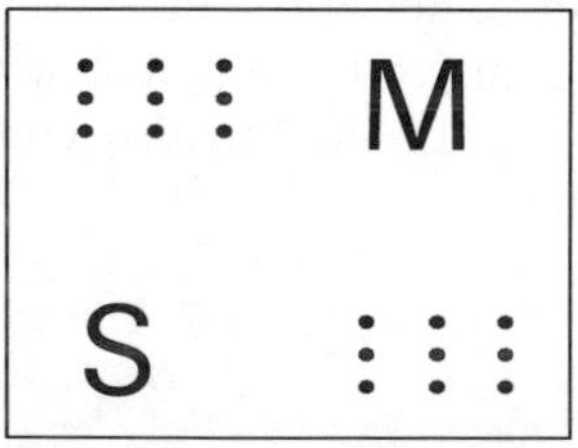

the participants received and through what they called 'consistent' and 'varied' mapping conditions. In the former, target and irrelevant items were from different categories, in the latter they could be from the same categories.

Results showed that in the consistent mapping condition it made little difference how many targets there were and how they were located. Only exposure time seemed to make a difference. Under the varied mapping condition the number of the targets and their locations made a difference as well. Schneider and Shiffrin's explanation was that in the consistent mapping condition the task was easy enough for automatic processing to be employed. In the varied condition participants had to use controlled processing, conducting a serial search through all the items in a frame.

A great deal of further research was inspired by Schneider and Shiffrin. Fisher (1984), for instance, suggested that there were clear limits to the number of items which could be processed simultaneously. This might not be much greater than the four items which Schneider and Shiffrin showed in each frame.

Feature Integration Theory

Treisman has taken this distinction between automatic and controlled attention further in what she calls **feature integration** theory. She distinguished **pre-attentive processing** and **focused attention**.

Pre-attentive Processing

With pre-attentive processing the individual scans and registers features right across the visual field, using parallel processing. This is, therefore, not unlike what Schneider and Shiffrin called automatic processing.

Focused Attention

In **focused attention** by contrast, the individual identifies objects one at a time, by serial processing. Treisman and Gelade (1980) examined pre-attentive processing as compared to focused attention. Where there were isolated features to be looked for, where the target differed from surrounding irrelevant items in colour, size or orientation, it would seem to pop out of the display automatically. How many items there were altogether was immaterial. Try the following exercise.

Exercise

Task A: Use marking pens with clear bright colours, say red and green. On a plain piece of white paper make 30 red X's and one green X and in a random array.
Task B: On a second sheet make 12 red X's, and one green X. Ask a friend to scan both sheets to locate the green X. Did it take longer to locate the target among 30 or among 12 irrelevant items?
Task C: Now make an array composed of 15 red X's, 15 green O's and one green X. Again ask your friend to locate the green X. Did it take longer to locate the target in this array?

In task *A* and task *B* the target would seem to pop out at you. It will not make much difference whether there are 12 or 30 items. You are looking for an isolated feature and can therefore use pre-attentive processing. However, in task *C* you are looking for a combination of two features, X and green. You cannot search at feature level but must search for a particular object, a more complex task. The more features there are, the longer it takes.

Kahneman's Capacity Theory of Attention

It is clear from the above research that some tasks require more attention than others. In some cases there is automatic processing, in others attention has to be focused. Allport *et al.* (1972) and Shaffer (1975) in research described earlier (p. 15) suggested that attention might be divided. Shiffrin and Schneider (1977, 1984) suggested that the distinction might be between automatic and controlled (or focused) attention. Underwood's (1974) experiment, also mentioned on p. 14, had hinted that there was a distinction between practised and unpractised performance. In real life, we can see this distinction. Driving a car on an uncluttered road, we are often able to listen to the radio or hold a conversation at the same time as driving competently. However, when the road conditions become difficult we need to turn off the radio and stop talking to focus all our attention on the task of driving. There seems to be an overall limitation on our capacity for attention. Kahneman (1973) suggested that there exists a central processor to co-ordinate and allocate our attentional resources (see Figure 2.5).

Broadbent (1977) had suggested something similar in response to Allport's work, that there was what he termed a **general executive controller**. Kahneman's idea was that this central processor dealt with resource allocation. Instead of a single channel, processing one thing at a time, there was an array of processing resources to be deployed flexibly. The factors determining the allocation of resources include: (a) the mental effort required; and (b) A person's level of arousal. More capacity was seen to be available when arousal levels were high. Arousal refers to a person's physiological state of alertness. This will be determined by:

1. The overall level of stimulation in the environment at the time.
2. A person's natural disposition (a neurotic person will be more easily aroused than a stable one).
3. Circadian rhythms. These are daily cycles of activity within a person's physiological system. There are times in the day when

---

FIGURE 2.5

Kahneman's Capacity Model of Attention

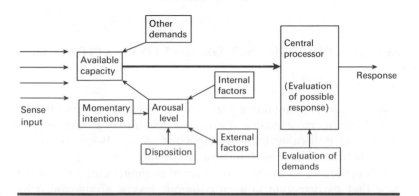

physiological functions such as heart rate, metabolic rate, breathing rate and body temperature are at their lowest (usually in the early hours of the morning) and times when they are at a maximum (in the late afternoon and early evening for many people).

4. Momentary intentions and enduring dispositions. The central processor is more likely to allocate resources to activities related to a person's immediate goals. Individuals will naturally turn their attention towards some external stimuli rather than others.

This seems to be a far more flexible system than that envisaged by Broadbent. In everyday life, there are both external and internal factors which determine whether we pay attention to something. An external stimulus, such as a cry for help, might grab our attention. But external demands will need to override the internal factors such as the immediate goals we have set ourselves to achieve and our enduring dispositions (the kind of people we are).

Self-assessment Questions

1. What conclusions did Schneider and Shiffrin come to as a result of their experiments?
2. Describe Treisman's 'feature integration' theory. How did it extend Schneider and Shiffrin's work?
3. Kahneman introduced the idea of resource allocation into selective attention. What factors did he see as influencing this allocation of resources, and what factors influenced the amount of resources available at any one time?

SECTION III   VIGILANCE OR SUSTAINED ATTENTION

Introduction

The problem of maintaining attention on something we find boring is familiar to most people. Early research into vigilance performance, as it became known, originated in the 1940s. With the introduction of radar **performance decrement**, as it became known, it was obviously serious because it could endanger life. It is still the case that participation in a monotonous task is accompanied by lowered performance, which gets worse the longer one is engaged on it. Motorway driving, for instance, when it is uneventful can result in poorer driving skills.

Early Research

Mackworth in the 1940s used three types of experimental technique to examine performance decrement:

1. The radar test. Participants were made to sit and watch a radar screen for occasional signals, visual blips, presented against a background of visual 'noise', random, non-signal visual events.
2. An auditory listening task. Participants were made to listen for sound tones, presented every 18 seconds for a duration of 2.5 seconds.
3. The clock test. This 'clock' had one pointer which moved in jumps at regular intervals, but every so often made a double jump. It could also be set to move continuously but occasionally speed up or slow down.

Participants had to respond by pressing a button or reporting signals verbally when each of these 'events' occurred. Experimenters recorded the **latency** of responses (the delay between the signal and the operator responding to it), **error rates**, and finally **evoked cortical responses** (measurements of the brain's activity taken by means of an **electroencephalogram (EEG)**).

Some Results of Early Research

The factors which seemed to affect performance included the following:

1. Aspects of the signal itself, its intensity, rate of presentation, regularity, duration and spatial arrangement. Better vigilance performance resulted from increases in the intensity, frequency and duration of the signal. Presenting the signals regularly or near the centre of the display also improved performance.
2. Knowledge of results. Where participants were given information on how well they had performed, even if this information was false, performance decrement was reduced.

3. Stimulation. Having a telephone in the room ringing at intervals, or having other people in the room, especially if they were of high status reduced performance decrement. For example, having officers in the room, when the participants were 'other ranks'.
4. Stimulant drugs such as amphetamines, administered in moderate doses, reduced performance decrement.
5. Personality. Highly introverted participants (as measured by Eysenck's Personality Inventory) showed almost no performance decrement.

Theories of Vigilance Decrement

Pavlovian Inhibition Theory (Mackworth, 1950)

Pavlov had researched what became known as classical conditioning in the 1920s. Dogs were presented with meat powder which caused them to salivate. This was the unconditional stimulus (UCS). The salivation was termed the unconditional response (UCR). This UCS was then paired with (presented at the same time as) a second stimulus, a bell or a buzzer, perhaps, which was known as the conditional stimulus (CS). After a number of such pairings, salivation was produced by presenting the CS alone. This was the conditional response (CR), produced by the reinforcement of the CS by UCS. After a number of such single (unreinforced) presentations the CR tended to die away. Extinction had occurred.

Mackworth's theory attempted to place the phenomenon of vigilance decrement within this framework. The conditional stimulus was the signal, the conditional response was key pressing. Knowledge of results (KR) provided reinforcement. It was suggested that extinction occurred as a result of a prolonged period without KR.

Criticisms of Pavlovian Inhibition Theory

Classical conditioning does not fit well with Mackworth's theory for several reasons:

1. It is not easy to believe that KR would act as a stimulus to produce key pressing.

2. Extinction in classical conditioning is the result of the inhibition of responses because UCS has not been paired with CS for a number of trials. In a vigilance task, vigilance decrement never reaches the point where there is no response to the signal at all.
3. In Pavlovian conditioning a large number of unpaired (CS without UCS) trials produces extinction, whatever the time-scale. In vigilance tasks, when the signal is presented more often the decrement declines.

Arousal Level Theory

It seems more plausible to link the performance decrement observed by Mackworth to participants' arousal level. In crude terms this is the degree of individuals' alertness. In physiological terms, though, it amounts to the level of activity in the brain (in the cortex, in subcortical structures such as the hypothalamus and in the autonomic nervous system).

Measurement of Arousal Level

The degree of activity in the cortex may be measured by means of an electroencephalogram (EEG). Electrodes are attached to a person's scalp and the potential difference measured between two electrodes, amplified and recorded on a continuous roll. When a person is relaxing with the eyes closed, it is possible to detect what are known as alpha rhythms (regular waves at about 8–12 cycles per second). When the person is attending to the world with eyes open, beta rhythms can be detected (less regular waves of lower amplitude and a frequency of 12–30 cycles per second).

Stroh (1971) recorded the alpha rhythms of participants during a one hour visual vigilance task. He wanted to find out the relationship between the level of alpha activity before a stimulus was presented and the likelihood of detecting it. If alpha activity is an indication of arousal level he could see whether arousal was a factor in vigilance decrement.

Stroh had 24 participants in his study in three groups:

A those whose alpha activity before a missed signal was lower than before a detected signal;

B   those whose alpha activity was lower before a detected signal; and
C   those for whom there was no difference.

Looking for other ways in which the groups differed he discovered that Group A were younger and more neurotic (as measured on personality inventories). Group B were older and less neurotic. Alpha rhythms are replaced by more complex beta rhythms as attention is engaged. A decrease in alpha goes with an increase in cortical arousal. While a spontaneous increase in arousal seems to improve the performance of older and less neurotic people, the reverse is true in younger and more neurotic individuals.

Factors Influencing Arousal Level

The factors which influence arousal level may be either **endogenous** (coming from within the individual), or **exogenous** (those from outside the individual):

1.   Endogenous factors include an individual's personality (particularly neuroticism) and **circadian rhythms** (the natural daily variation in physiological and psychological performance).
2.   Exogenous factors include:
     (a)   Drives and incentives. Hunger, thirst and pain are examples, as well as the anticipation of pleasure or pain.
     (b)   Environmental circumstances. Noise and bright lights may increase arousal (remember that Mackworth found that a telephone ringing occasionally lowered vigilance decrement). The higher the intensity, the greater the arousal. Colour may influence arousal also: blue is less stimulating than red.
     (c)   Surprising or novel events.
     (d)   Drugs. Amphetamines or caffeine may raise arousal; alcohol or barbiturates may lower it.
     (e)   The difficulty of the task. The harder a task, the greater the arousal.

To sum up, it has been suggested that there was an optimum level of arousal for effective performance. A variety of factors may influence arousal levels. A neurotic individual looking forward with anxiety to an examination misses the bus and arrives late. The supervisor appears annoyed and the paper is difficult. Such a level of arousal is piled up from various sources so that performance is drastically impaired. Figure 2.6 illustrates the relationship between arousal and performance.

This has become known as the Yerkes–Dodson Law (Yerkes and Dodson, 1908). As arousal increases, so does performance up to an optimum level. If arousal continues to increase beyond this level performance deteriorates.

Individual Differences and Vigilance

Other indices of arousal (besides EEG) include **galvanic skin response (GSR)**, **pulse rate** and **pupil diameter**. As with EEG studies in relation to vigilance there is contradictory evidence. Sometimes there are higher, sometimes lower GSR changes or pulse rates before a missed signal on a vigilance task. This can be explained in terms of individual differences. Kahneman (1973) has argued that pupil diameter is a good indicator of cortical arousal, but this has not been tested in relation to vigilance.

It has been suggested that extroverts are chronically under-aroused and this is the reason why they perform less well on

---

FIGURE 2.6

The Relationship between Arousal and Performance (Yerkes–Dodson Law)

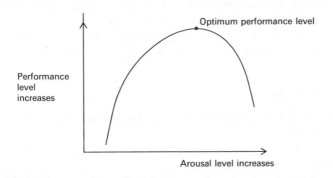

vigilance tasks. Their extroversion manifests itself in stimulus-seeking to spur on their reluctant arousal systems. When a vigilance task becomes monotonous and the novelty wears off, then their sustained attention is less.

Evoked Cortical Responses

Evoked cortical responses (ECR) are tiny electrical changes which occur in the cortex when stimuli are presented to a person. They occur equally with all the senses. Haider *et al.* (1964) carried out an interesting study of ECR in relation to a vigilance task. Light flashes were presented to participants at three second intervals. Some of these flashes were dimmer than others and constituted the signals in the experiment. Participants responded by key pressing. As the experiment progressed, the latency (the time-gap between the signal and the ECR) of the evoked responses increased. Where signals were missed ECR's were smaller and their latency was greater.

Wilkinson *et al.* (1966) took this further. There seemed to be four components of ECR, two positive and two negative micro-volt deflections. Before missed signals there seemed to be a larger second negative deflection and the first negative deflection had greater latency than in the case of detected signals.

Conclusion

Research seems to suggest that vigilance decrement is related to a lowering of arousal levels when a person is engaged in a boring task. Performance on this kind of task may in turn be related to such factors as an individual's personality, the time of day, and exogenous factors such as stimulation and the use of drugs.

Self-assessment Questions

1. What were the three types of vigilance test which Mackworth examined?
2. What factors seemed to reduce the viglance decrement on a long and monotonous task?

3. Define what is meant by 'arousal'. What appears to be the relationship between arousal and performance on a vigilance task?
4. Describe two ways of measuring arousal.

FURTHER READING

M. W. Matlin, *Cognition* (Fort Worth: Holt, Rinehart & Winston, 1989).

M. W. Eysenck, *A Handbook of Cognitive Psychology* (Hillsdale, N.J.: Lawrence Erlbaum, 1984).

J. Radford and E. Govier (eds), *A Textbook of Psychology*, 2nd edition (London: Routledge, 1991).

34

Perception 3

At the end of this chapter you should be able to:

1. Distinguish between sensation and perception.
2. Outline some of the factors (such as 'set', emotion and motivation) which may determine how the world around us is perceived.
3. Describe how information about a three-dimensional world is processed and how we perceive depth.
4. Describe how objects are perceived and recognised. In particular, indicate what is meant by 'perceptual constancy'.
5. Evaluate some of the evidence which indicates whether perception is innate or learned.

INTRODUCTION

This chapter describes how information from the three-dimensional, 'real' world, received through our senses, is processed to provide a basis for our interaction with the environment. The focus will be upon visual perception, though much of what is discussed applies equally to the other senses. Perception can be said to be the process by which data from the environment is interpreted to allow us to make sense of it.

As Gregory says:

Perception is not determined simply by stimulus patterns; rather it is a dynamic searching for the best interpretation of the available data (Gregory, 1966).

SECTION I   THE PHYSIOLOGICAL BASIS FOR VISUAL PERCEPTION

The primary point of contact between ourselves and the world around us is sensation. Sources of information fall into two categories:

1. **Exteroceptors**, which provide information about our external environment and consist particularly of our senses, sight, hearing, touch, taste and smell.
2. **Interoceptors**, which provide information about our internal environment and include:
   (a) **Receptors** (organs of sensation) which provide information about our internal state, directly about our body chemistry, and indirectly about our motivational and emotional states. For example, if we are upset emotionally, changes occur in our body chemistry – the distribution of the blood, for instance, which provide us with information about this upset.
   (b) **Kinaesthetic receptors** in our muscles, which provide information about our movements, and in the vestibular system (centring upon the semicircular canals in the inner ear) which provide information about head movements.

The focus in this section will be upon the visual sense. Eyes provide primary visual information, each providing slightly different information from the other. They are, after all, 7–8 cms apart. The overall structure of the eye is described in Figure 3.1.

Light enters the eye through the **cornea**, its transparent outer covering, and is focused on the **retina** (in particular on the most sensitive area of the retina, the **fovea**). This focusing is achieved in part through the cornea and in part through the lens altering its shape. When the ciliary muscles are relaxed, the lens becomes a rounder ellipse: when they are contracted the lens becomes a less round, thinner ellipse (see Figure 3.2). This process is called **accommodation**.

The sense receptors in the human eye are composed of two kinds of light sensitive cells, rods and cones. There are about 130 million rods and about 6 million cones.

FIGURE 3.1

Diagram Representing the Eye

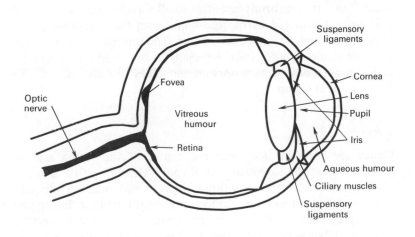

FIGURE 3.2

The Lens and Ciliary Muscles

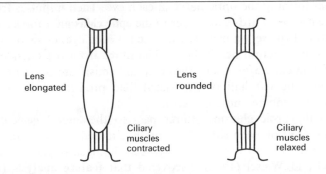

Rods

Rods are receptors specialised for the reception of low levels of light. They contain **rhodopsin**, a visual pigment highly sensitive to light which it converts into neural energy, which is acceptable to the brain. They are uniformly sensitive to all wavelengths of light and uniformly distributed across the retina with the exception of the blind spot, which has no rods or cones. They enable us to have very sensitive monochrome vision especially in low light conditions (at night vision tends to be monochrome). They are also responsible for peripheral vision.

Cones

Cones are concentrated near the centre of the retina and in particular near the fovea (or yellow spot). They are of three types, each specialised for the reception of light in particular wavelengths of the visible spectrum: one for low wavelength light (at the red end of the spectrum); one for the middle region of the spectrum; and the third to higher wavelength light (the violet end of the spectrum). They therefore enable us to see colour. While the rods become overloaded in the high light conditions of daylight, the cones are not sensitive to low levels of illumination and require daylight to function.

Optical Nerve Pathways

Nerve impulses are transmitted through **bipolar cells** and **retinal ganglions** forming the optic nerve in each eye. Then impulses from each eye travel towards each other to the **optic chiasma**. Fibres from the halves of the retina nearest the nose (in each eye) cross over to the opposite cerebral hemisphere while fibres from the outside of the retina in each eye pass to the cerebral hemisphere on the same side. Thus the left half of the visual field projects to the right cerebral hemisphere and vice versa.

From the optic chiasma, fibres pass to the **lateral geniculate nucleus (LGN)** on each side of the brain, situated in the **thalamus**, and from the LGN to the **visual cortex** at the back of the brain.

Hubel and Wiesel (1962) discovered that **feature analysis** (the interpretation of features in the visual field) takes place in the

primary visual cortex (V1). Individual cells respond to bars of light of particular orientation. Different cells respond to different orientations. These are called **simple cells**. In addition there are **complex** cells, with a larger field, again responsive to light at a particular angle but only when moved to and fro. **Hypercomplex cells** respond to bars of a particular orientation when moving, but only when they are of a specific length. Information about light intensity and contours is also processed by the simple, complex and hypercomplex cells. This process is also referred to in Section II of this chapter under the heading of pattern recognition.

Differences in the stimulation between one eye and the other (**retinal disparity**), colour and movement are registered in secondary areas of the visual cortex (V2–V5) (Wade and Swanston, 1991).

Colour Vision

Colour vision occurs in response to the cones in the retina. There are three types of cone (Marks *et al.*, 1964):

1. blue sensitive;
2. green sensitive;
3. red sensitive.

The colour of the light is analysed in terms of how much blue, green or red light it contains. This is termed a **trichromat process**. In the LGN the light is recoded in a different way. This **opponent process**, as it is called, depends upon four types of specialised cell:

1. Those which increase their activity with red light, but decrease it with green.
2. Those which do the opposite (increase activity with green light and decrease with red).
3. Those which increase activity with blue light but decrease activity with yellow.
4. Those which increase activity with yellow light but decrease with blue.

This opponent process theory (de Valois *et al.*, 1966) is related to the theory of colour vision developed by Hering in 1878. The trichromat theory goes back to Young and von Helmholtz in the nineteenth century.

Evidence for Colour Vision Theories

1. The fact that white light can be generated by mixing blue, green and red light tends to support the trichromat theory.
2. After prolonged stimulation by a particular colour, after-images can be seen in the opposing colour. Try this exercise.

Exercise

Fix your eyes on a square of red paper for, say, 30 seconds, then turn them on to a blank sheet. What do you see? Then try green, blue and yellow squares.

After the red square you should expect to see a green after-image, after the green, red; the blue, yellow and the yellow, blue. This seems to lend support to the opponent process theory.

3. Colour blindness also lends support to the opponent process theory. Those with normal vision see combinations of red-green, blue-yellow and black and white. Those who are red-green colour blind cannot differentiate between red and green. This would suggest a deficiency of specialised red-green cells in the LGN. Similarly, much rarer yellow-blue colour blind people cannot differentiate yellow and blue. Both are called dichromats. Rarely, there are also monochromats who cannot see colour at all.

Self-assessment Questions

1. What is the distinction between interoceptors and exteroceptors?
2. Describe the operation of rods and cones in the retina?
3. What is the function of the optic chiasma? Which area of the visual field registers on which side of the brain?

4. What is the significance of Hubel and Wiesel's discoveries in relation to the visual cortex? How does this relate to our ability to detect the features, say, of the letter A?
5. How do we see colour? Compare and evaluate trichromat and opponent process theories of colour vision.

SECTION II   SENSATION AND PERCEPTION

Introduction

Sensation relates to the collection of data from the environment by means of the senses. In Section I of this chapter there was a brief account of the way in which our eyes collect visual data. Perception relates to our interpretation of this data. It takes into account experiences stored in our memory, the context in which the sensation occurs and our internal state (our emotions and motivations).

Gregory (1966) has described this process as one of forming hypotheses about what the senses tell us. This section will deal with some of the ways in which this interpretation of data results in perception of the world. It will include **depth perception, recognition of objects**, and **perceptual constancies.**

Depth Perception

The world around us is three dimensional, but the data collected about the world through our senses is in two dimensions (a flat image on the retinas of our eyes). The interpretation of this data within the brain results in three-dimensional perception. This perception of depth depends on the brain's use of a number of clues. Some of these **cues**, as they are termed, use data from both eyes (binocular cues). Others use data from one eye only (monocular cues).

Binocular Cues to Depth Perception

1. Retinal disparity **Retinal disparity** refers to the slightly different view of the world registered by each eye. You can test this for yourself:

Exercise

Hold a pencil (or any other small object) in front of your eyes about 15 cms (6 inches) away from them. Close first your left eye, and look at the object with your right; then change eyes and look at the object with the left eye.

The view of the object you get with your right eye is slightly different from that which you get with the left. Retinal disparity, therefore, provides two sets of data which, interpreted together in the brain, provide **stereoscopic vision**, an apparent 3D image.

2. Convergence   **Convergence** is the movement of the eyes together so that each may focus upon an object. Try this exercise.

Exercise

Hold a pencil up in front of your eyes and gradually move it in towards them, while fixing your vision on it. Then move it away again.

You will feel your eyeballs turning inwards to follow its movement and the muscles of your eyes contracting. This sensation of muscle movement **(kinaesthetic sense)** provides data about how far the object is from your eyes. In other words about depth.

Monocular Cues to Depth

These monocular cues depend on data received from one eye only. Even with the loss of the sight of one eye, a person can still perceive the world in three dimensions. It is more difficult, though. You can appreciate this if you close one eye, go into another room and pick something up from a table. It will be more difficult to locate it.

Painters throughout history have used monocular cues to provide an impression of depth in a flat two-dimensional painting. These cues include:

1. **Linear perspective**. Parallel lines appear to come together as they recede into the distance. Figure 3.3 shows a building. You know that the part of the building on the right is further away than that on the left, because the lines of the roof, doors, windows and base of the building converge towards the right.
2. **Height in a horizontal plane**. Distant objects seem to be higher, nearer objects lower in the horizontal plane.
3. **Relative size**. The more distant they are, the smaller objects will appear to be. A painter who wants to create the impression of depth, may include figures of different sizes. The observer will assume that a human figure or some other well-known object is consistent in size and will see the smaller objects as more distant.
4. **Superimposition of objects.** Where an object is superimposed upon another (partly hiding it) the superimposed object will appear to be nearer.
5. **Clarity**. Objects which are nearer appear to be clearer and more well-defined than those in the distance.
6. **Light and shade**. Shadow has the effect of pushing darker parts of an image back. Highlights bring other parts forward, thus increasing the three-dimensional effect.
7. **Texture**. The coarser the texture of an image the closer it seems to be. If a pavement of bricks is to be depicted, the impression

---

FIGURE 3.3

An Illustration of Linear Perspective

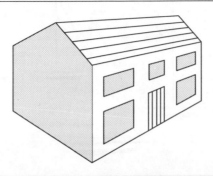

of depth is created by the texture of the bricks becoming finer as the pavement goes into the distance.

8. **Motion parallax**. As you move the apparent movement of objects past you will be slower, the more distant they are. On a wide open road, with few objects close at hand, a car will appear to those inside it to be going more slowly than on a narrow road with hedges or fences close at hand.

In the illustration (Figure 3.4) several monocular cues are illustrated. The texture of the wavelets on the sea appears finer as you go into the distance. Sailing boats appear smaller and higher in the horizontal plane the more distant they are and where one partially obscures another it appears to be closer.

The above monocular cues relate to features in the visual field itself and can be referred to as **secondary cues**.

9. **Accommodation**. As has been described earlier (p. 36) the lens of the eye alters its shape in order to focus the image more accurately on the retina. Ciliary muscles contract to elongate the lens and focus upon more distant objects, relax to allow it to become more rounded and focus upon nearer objects. Data is fed to the brain from kinaesthetic senses in these ciliary muscles, providing information about the nearness or distance of the object focused upon.

FIGURE 3.4

Some Monocular Cues to Depth Perception

Together with the binocular cues (retinal disparity and convergence) accommodation relates to the physiology of our visual processes and so can be described as **a primary cue**. None of these cues operates in isolation and it is their combination which provides the information enabling us to form a hypothesis about the view in front of us.

Perceptual Constancies

The world around us has the potential to provide total chaos and confusion as we perceive it. Images projected upon the retinas of our eyes from a single object vary so much that, if we depended only on data from this source, objects would have no constancy, but would appear to be different each time they were presented to us. That this does not occur is the result of perceptual constancy. Shape, size, brightness and colour, and location are all areas of perception in which this concept of constancy applies. We shall take each in turn.

1. **Shape constancy**. Objects project different shapes on our retinas according to the angle from which they are viewed. Try this:
Your drawings will look something like Figure 3.5.

Exercise

Take a tea cup and saucer, look at them directly from on top and with a pencil draw what you see. Then look at them again from the side and draw what you see. Compare your two drawings.

The appearance of the cup is totally different in each case. How do we recognise the images we receive? In the first view of the cup, there may be some difficulty in recognising it as a cup, less difficulty in the case of the side view. In each case, a hypothesis is made from the data received about what it is we are seeing. This hypothesis is tested and in most cases an appropriate response is made. Shape constancy enables us to recognise objects for what they are, even when the retinal image we receive varies.

FIGURE 3.5

An Illustration of Shape Constancy

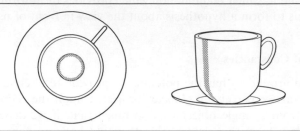

In some cases, though, there may be ambiguity and an inappropriate response may be made. The basis for these hypotheses is our experience of perceiving similar things before. In ambiguous cases, two alternative hypotheses may be made and it may be difficult to decide between them. This results in a visual illusion. Illusions are discussed in a later section of this chapter.

2. **Size constancy** This relates to the fact that the image of an object projected on the retinas of our eyes becomes smaller, the more distant the object is. Yet we know the real size of the object from experience and scale-up the perceived size of the object to take this into account. Try this:

Exercise

Hold a 10 pence piece 30 cms away from your eyes and then move it away to arms length. Does it appear to get smaller?

It is not noticeably smaller and yet the image it projects on the retinas of your eyes is smaller. We reach a compromise between the size we know the coin to be and the retinal size of it. How this compromise is arrived at depends on factors like our familiarity with the object and other cues comparing it with another object the size of which we know, for instance.

Perception of size is determined jointly by the retinal size of an object, and what can be called the **egocentric distance** between the observer's eyes and the object, that is to say the distance as it appears to the individual observer (Wade and Swanston, 1991).

Emmert's Law

The relationship between perceived size and retinal image may be summarised in the equation

$S = sD,$

where S is the perceived size of the object,
s is the retinal size and
D the egocentric distance.

This is called **Emmerts law**. The following demonstration will show how this works:

Exercise

Take a square of green coloured paper with a black dot in the centre. Stare at the dot for 30 seconds then turn your gaze to a blank sheet of white paper. You will see a red after-image (as has been shown earlier in this chapter on p. 40). After a few seconds, transfer your gaze to a white wall at a greater distance from you.

The size of the after-image will vary proportionately with the distance from the eye. That is, if the distance between the eye and the first after-image was 20 cms and the distance between the eye and the wall was 100 cms the second after-image will be five times the size of the first.

3. **Brightness and colour constancies**. The brightness of an object remains constant regardless of how it is illuminated. Experience tells us how light or dark an object is. Once we recognise it, experience will influence our perception of it. We know a piece of

black velvet is dark and it will remain so, however it is illuminated. But if light is projected on a piece of black velvet in such a way that there is no edge illuminated and we have no other cue to show that it is black velvet, it will appear light. Try this:

Exercise

Take a piece of grey paper about 10 cms square and place it in the centre of a sheet of white paper. Take another piece of the same grey paper and place it on a sheet of black paper. Put a piece of tracing paper over each sheet. Which square of grey paper appears lighter?

The square on the black background will appear to be lighter than it really is, the other darker.

Similarly, whatever the illumination, the colour of an object will appear to be what you know it to be. You know a cricket ball is red. It will still appear red, even under coloured illumination.

4. **Location constancy**. This is a similar phenomenon to the above. We have become accustomed to the locations of things around us in relation to ourselves. When our heads move, objects around us do not move although the image projected on our retinas changes. Experiments with distorting goggles go some way to explaining this. The best known is that of Stratton (1897). He fitted himself with glasses which inverted his visual field. At first, he experienced confusion, but after a few days he seemed to adapt and his location constancy seemed to be restored. When he finally took the glasses off he again needed some time to readjust.

Pattern Recognition

This is the heart of the relationship between perception and sensation. It relates closely to depth perception and perceptual constancy. Recognition of a word written on a page, or perhaps even more basically than this, of Grannie when we see her, depends on pattern recognition. There are four theories or models of pattern recognition. These include **template matching theory**, **prototype models**, **distinctive features models** and the **scene analysis approach**. This section will examine each in turn.

Template Matching Theory

In template matching theory, the stimulus is compared to a set of patterns stored in memory. It is then 'recognised' as the pattern it resembles most closely. For instance, it is suggested that we have a number of faces stored in memory of people we have met. When we meet someone, we mentally scan through these stored faces until we find one that closely resembles the face before us. Recognition then takes place. However, there are several problems with this theory.

1. The **template** has to fit exactly or the system will not work. Computer sorting operates in this way, but for it to work there have to be certain conditions:
   (a) The patterns have to be standardised. There are different ways of writing a letter A as in the figure below (Figure 3.6). For a computer to recognise it the letter must be written in exactly the form in which has been stored in the computer.
   (b) The patterns also have to be very well differentiated. A number 1 that looks rather like a 7 will not do.

It is evident that the patterns which humans need to recognise are much more flexible. We need to be able to recognise Grannie whatever she is wearing, whatever kind of hair-do she has. Pattern recognition theory needs to accommodate the fact that we are able consistently to recognise Grannie, however she looks and the letter A, no matter how it is written.

FIGURE 3.6

A Number of Ways of Writing the Letter A

A a A *a* A a

---

2. There would need to be an infinite number of templates stored for us to recognise all possible variations in letters, let alone faces and other shapes. There are clearly storage problems.

3. The procedure envisaged by the theory would be very time consuming. In order to recognise a letter we should need to scan mentally through all the stored templates, and yet it is possible to read 200 words a minute. Supposing an average of five letters in a word, and, say, a dozen templates for each letter, there would be 12 000 templates to scan each minute, a formidable task.

4. There are likely to be difficulties, also, when images are rotated. Pinker (1984) notes that when shapes are rotated the image on the retina changes drastically. Every time the shape was rotated, there would need to be another template. Yet Jolicoeur and Landau (1984) estimate that when an image is rotated 180 degrees it requires only 15 milliseconds of processing time to recognise it.

5. There is also the problem of recognition of parts of shapes. It is possible to recognise a shape, even when only a fragment is registered on the retina. For this theory to work, there would need to be templates of a whole series of parts of objects.

Given all these problems, template matching theory does not seem capable of explaining the phenomenon of pattern recognition.

Prototype Models

This seems to relate to Plato's theory of ideas (*Republic*, Book X). This suggests that objects in the world around are in a sense reflections of idealised prototypes and it is these prototypes which are stored in memory. When a shape is encountered it is compared with a prototype. If the match is close enough, (it does not need to be exact) recognition takes place.

Research has shown this approach to be a more useful one than template matching. Franks and Bransford (1971) asked participants in their study to draw transformations of prototype designs which differed in varying degrees from the original. Shown the original prototype design, they were confident that they had seen it before, even though it had not been presented to them. This confidence varied with the closeness of the resemblance between the transformation and the prototype.

Prototype models do seem to get over some of the difficulties in the template theory. They explain how shapes may be recognised even with different orientations and representations, but it seems to be a philosophical approach rather than one based upon reality. Spoehr and Lehmkuhler (1982) suggested that there might be a need for templates of prototypes!

Feature Analysing Models

In feature analysing models, features of objects or patterns which have been encountered before are stored in memory rather than templates or prototypes. They have their origin in Selfridge's (1959) **pandemonium model**. This was a computer program originally designed to recognise the patterns of dots and dashes in the Morse code, and extended by Lindsay and Norman (1972) to form a model of how the brain might recognise letters. Selfridge hypothesiscd **demons** which 'shriek in the presence of the feature they represent'. The first level of 'demons' represents line features, a vertical line for instance; the second level represents angles or the points where two lines meet; the third level of demons represent possible patterns; and finally there is a decision demon. The loudness of the demons' shrieks indicates the degree of certainty that the feature is present.

Gibson's (1969) research showed that people take longer to differentiate between similar letters such as B and R than dissimilar letters such as X and O. The former have many similar features, the latter relatively few.

Garner (1979) presented participants with one-letter targets followed by a series of letters one at a time. They had to press one key if the letter was the same as the target, another key if it was different. All 26 letters were used as targets with 50–75 trials for each target. Where letters had many different features, participants required a shorter time to make their decisions than where there were many similar features.

This seems to tie up with the neurological research by Hubel and Wiesel described earlier in this chapter (pp. 38–9) (Hubel, 1982; Hubel and Wiesel, 1965; 1979). They showed that individual neurons in the visual cortex responded to different line orientations. There are also some relationships with Treisman and Gelade's feature integration theory outlined in Chapter 2 (pp. 23–4).

Scene Analysis Approach

There are characteristics both of feature analysis and prototypes in the scene analysis approach. As so often in cognitive psychology there has been an attempt to develop computer-based theories to accomplish the perceptual tasks that human observers perform. This use of computers to simulate human perception is known as **machine vision**. Computer scientists, interested in **artificial intelligence (AI)**, have studied not only how perception occurs in humans but also how any organism or any machine perceives. At the present time, however, AI falls far short of full understanding of human perception. As Ullman says:

> The proficiencies of the human system in analysing spatial information far surpass the capacities of current artificial systems (Ullman, 1984, p. 97).

Human perceivers are able to recognise incomplete objects in a way which is not possible for computers. An example of the scene analysis approach is Biederman's **recognition by components theory** (Biederman, 1987). Presented with an unfamiliar object or pattern people will segment it to see if any part is familiar. Biederman suggests that this process of **segmentation** occurs with any object we see, familiar or unfamiliar. There are three stages in the recognition of objects:

1. Surface characteristics are registered, such as patterns of light and dark. A line drawing of the object can result.
2. Segmentatation then occurs, particularly in the concave regions of the object.
3. The component parts are then matched with representations in memory. Numerous possible representations may be scanned simultaneously by parallel processing. Matching may be either partial or complete.

This approach is a very complex one, too new as yet for much critical analysis to have been made, but clearly it initiates a change in the way in which pattern recognition is studied.

The Importance of Context in Pattern Recognition

In reality, shapes, objects and letters do not occur in isolation but in context and this context has an important bearing on their recognition.

Chapter 1 described differences between top down and bottom up processing. Most of the theories and approaches to pattern recognition have concentrated upon **bottom-up** processing. Emphasis has been on the stimulus, whether it is a template that needs to be matched or a set of features to be analysed. A **top-down** approach starts with people's concepts and expectations. Patterns can be recognised easily and rapidly, because we expect certain shapes to be found in certain locations. The process of reading illustrates this. If one or more letters are obscured or omitted altogether from a word in the text there is usually not much dif-icu-ty in re-di-g it. If an additional word is inserted we may not notice that it is there:

> DOGS ARE NOT
> ALLOWED IN THE
> THE PARK

The redundant THE is often not noticed at all. Some of the newer computer models of pattern detection (McClelland and Rumelhart (1981), for example) allow the computer to change its mind in the light of the context. Where an obviously impossible word results from the system's analysis, it can backtrack to test whether the features might equally represent a less impossible word. But while it is possible for a computer to allow for context in a word, to do the same for a word in the context of a sentence is too difficult so far.

Self-assessment Questions

1. Briefly describe the distinction between 'sensation' and 'perception'.
2. List two binocular and three monocular cues to depth perception and describe each briefly.
3. What is meant by perceptual constancy? Describe the way in which size constancy scaling operates.
4. List four theories which have attempted to explain pattern recognition. Say which seems to you to be the most satisfactory. Give some reasons for your choice.

SECTION III   THEORIES, MODELS AND PRINCIPLES

This section discusses a number of theories which have been advanced about the relationship between sensation and perception. These theories will include Gestalt theories of perceptual organisation, Gibson's direct theory of perception and Neisser's cyclical theory.

Gestalt Theories of Perception

The Gestalt psychologists, principally Köhler, Koffka, and Wertheimer, working in the 1920s and 1930s suggested that there existed within the brain an innate capacity for **organising perceptions**, which followed certain rules. The 'whole' of perception was more than the sum of the parts, that is to say, the sum of all the individual sensations an individual receives. To begin with they were interested to explore what makes figures stand out against a background (the distinction between **figure and ground**). They maintained that there were **laws of organisation** which determined the way in which individuals perceived things. Electrical fields within the brain were responsible for this organisation, so that there was automatic perception of 'good' figures. Where the figure/ ground distinction was ambiguous, the electrical fields switched from one interpretation to another. The basic principle on which Gestalt organisation depended was the **Law of Prägnanz**. This may be defined as **good form**. Koffka (1935) expressed it as follows:

> Psychological organisation will always be as 'good' as the prevailing conditions allow.

Perhaps this rather abstract notion of 'good form' may be interpreted as that which is intuitively satisfying.

The other principles (or laws) amount to explanation of this principle of Prägnanz. These laws rarely operate in isolation, frequently complementing or even opposing each other. They include the following:

1. **Proximity**. Elements in an array which are close together are taken as belonging together. In the illustration (Figure 3.7) you can see three groups of two vertical lines. They would not naturally be seen as six individual independent lines.

FIGURE 3.7

Gestalt Laws of Perception (Proximity)

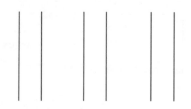

2. **Similarity**. Elements which are similar tend to be grouped together. Below in Figure 3.8 is a row of six circles. They will naturally be seen as pairs, two pairs of black circles and two pairs of white ones.

FIGURE 3.8

Gestalt Laws of Perception (Similarity)

3. **Closure**. An incomplete figure will tend to be seen as a complete one. In Figure 3.9 a is a square. At least, that is how it appears. It is still seen as a square in spite of breaks in each side. A word with one or more letters obscured can still be read as in Figure 3.9b, because the principle of closure will tend to complete it.
4. **Continuity**. Where figures are defined by a single unbroken line they tend to be seen as an entity. In Figure 3.10 you will tend to see two continuous curved lines rather than two pointed figures meeting at A.

FIGURE 3.9

Gestalt Laws of Perception (Closure)

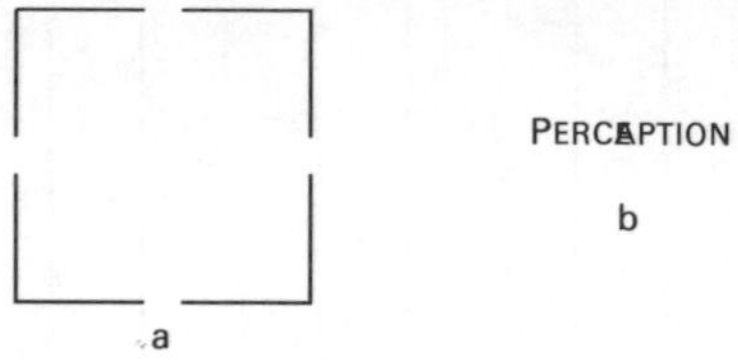

PERCEPTION

b

a

FIGURE 3.10

Gestalt Laws of Perception (Continuity)

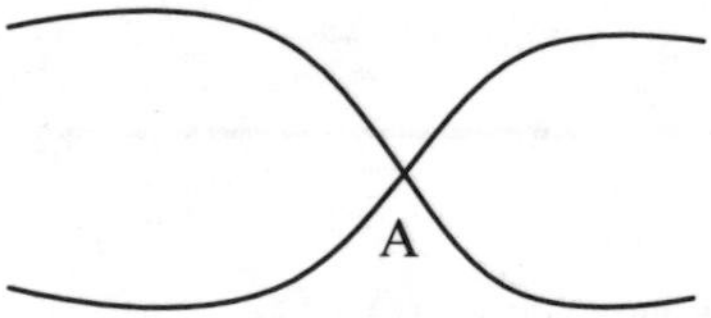

A

Attempts have been made to test these Gestalt laws empirically. In one experiment Pomerantz (1981) showed participants dots which they could join up as they liked. The prediction was that when the participants were shown patterns of dots suggesting simple figures of 'good form', all the participants would join them up in a sim-ilar way and the resultant figures would be 'good' ones which observed Gestalt laws of organisation. Where the dot patterns did not suggest 'good' figures there would be much more variation in the ways in which they were joined up. This turned out to be the case.

Eysenck (1984) criticises Gestalt principles as being merely descriptive and having no explanatory power. They are also limited in that they only directly applicable to two-dimensional representation.

Gregory's Theory of Perception

Gregory (1972) took the view that the process of perception was an active one. Data received from the senses resulted in a **perceptual hypothesis** being set up. An individual's experience of the world and expectations resulting from that experience provided the means to test the hypothesis. The perceptual hypothesis was a 'first guess' at what the sensory data meant, based upon experience. For instance, experience suggests that more distant objects appear smaller. If there are cues in the sensory data to suggest something is distant (perspective cues for instance, as in the Ponzo illusion, illustrated on p. 67), and if senses show it to be the same size as something apparently closer, then the perceptual hypothesis will be that it is larger, hence the illusion. Experience, context, motivations, emotional content all provide the means for us to test the provisional hypothesis which has been set up. This is a top-down process.

Gibson's Theory of Direct Perception

Gibson (1986) has argued that there need not be processing stages interposed between the light falling on the retina and the responses made by the organism as a result. This is **direct perception**. The theory stressed the function of the senses as a means of providing for individuals all the information needed to enable them to interact with the environment. Individuals have what Gibson terms an **ambient optical array**, which consists of all the light rays which converge on the retina. For instance, as a person moves from a sitting to a standing position this ambient optical array will change, providing new information about the environment as a basis for action. Objects in the environment will appear larger or smaller and will have different textual gradients depending on distance. It is this ambient optical array which provides direct sensory information rather than there being a need for the brain to interpret incoming data in the light of experience. Processing of the information is not done cognitively but at a neural level. It is the whole array in front of you which provides the information necessary for you to act. When there is an illusion, it is just that the information in the array is insufficient for an appropriate response.

There are disadvantages with this **ecological approach**, as it has been called:

1. Gibson concentrated on the activation of the visual system as a whole, but he did not make clear how the inputs were transformed into visual perceptions.
2. It seems more suitable as an explanation of innately-programmed reactions to environmental circumstances. The visual array triggers stereotyped activity directly. A wasp buzzes against a closed window pane in reaction to a total visual environment.
3. Eysenck (1984) has suggested that the theory is in a sense too good. Visual stimulation provides so much information that perception should normally be perfect. But this is clearly not always the case. The tendency of large objects at great distances to look much smaller than they actually are is a case in point.

Neisser's Cyclical Theory of Perception

Neisser's (1976) **cyclical theory** could be described as a combination of top-down and bottom-up processing theory. He saw perceivers as starting with a perceptual model. On the basis of **sensory cues**, a person's expectations were used to build a model of probable objects. This perceptual model consisted of likely objects or events represented mentally. This model was then tested against sensory cues in the environment; the individual instituted an active search for cues which would either confirm or confound the model. This active search consisted of a bottom-up analysis of sensory information, as a result of which the model might need to be revised. There was thus an interaction between top-down or **concept driven** processing, where the individual's concepts and expectations led and bottom-up or **data driven** processing.

The term which Neisser used for this approach is **analysis-by-synthesis**. The cycle consists of the generation of a **perceptual model** (synthesis), extracting information about the environment in order to correct and update the model (analysis) and repeating the process continuously to monitor the environment using expectations derived from previous experiences. Figure 3.11 shows this process.

Neisser combined the construction of hypotheses based upon experience and expectations of what the environment might be like, with the extraction from the environment of cues to enable the observer to correct the hypothesis in the light of data extracted.

FIGURE 3.11

Neisser's Cyclical Theory of Perception

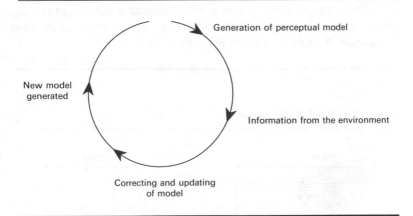

Expectations are constantly changing. Neisser's models provide for a continuous exploration of the environment in order to confirm, modify, or confound expectations. Gombrich (1960) spoke of the **beholder's share** in relation to the appreciation of works of art. Neisser's view has something in common with this. The sense that each person makes of the world is different from that of every other person.

Brunswik's Model

Brunswik's (1956) model seems to have something in common with Gibson's theory in that it links perception very closely with action. Its central point is the organism (O). To one side are the inputs into the perceptual process, first distal inputs (c) which will include such things as a person's experiences, motivations, emotional states and personality disposition. Closer to the event, proximal inputs (b) include its context in terms of the physical objects surrounding it and the immediate sensory stimulation which constitutes the basis for perception (the interpretation of what has gone before). Beyond this perception, on the response side, is the establishment of a response set: for instance, the physiological changes which accompany any emotion generated by the event (increases in heart rate, muscular tension etc). This is called molecular and is followed by action (molar) response (B) and finally the future consequences of the event (C). These might include the emotional consequences, practical precautions taken, increased awareness, etc. For a schematic diagram of Brunswik's model see Figure 3.12.

FIGURE 3.12

Brunswik's Model of Perception

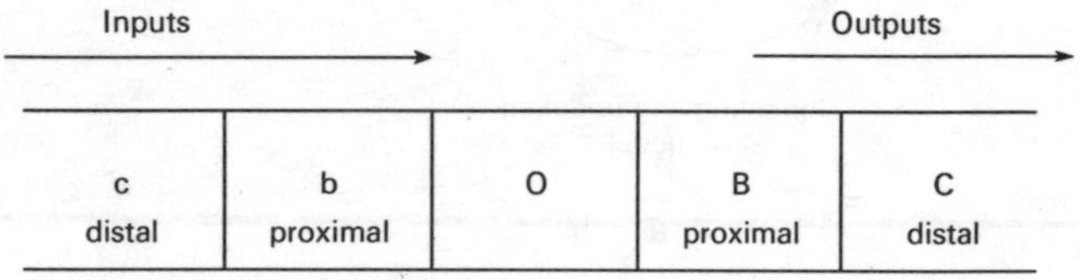

Inputs			Outputs	
c	b	O	B	C
distal	proximal		proximal	distal

Set as an Explanatory Concept

Set is a portmanteau term for a whole range of emotional, motivational, social and cultural factors which can have an influence upon cognition. As such it helps to explain why we perceive the world around us in the way we do.

Set predisposes an individual towards particular perceptions. It may be induced by emotional, motivational, social or cultural factors. Its effects include:

1. Readiness: set involves an enhanced readiness to respond to a signal.
2. Attention: set involves a priority processing channel. The expected stimulus will be processed ahead of everything else.
3. Selection: set involves the selection of one stimulus in preference to others.
4. Interpretation: the expected signal is already interpreted before it occurs. The individual knows beforehand what to do when the stimulus is picked up.

An athlete waiting for the starting gun hears 'get set' and each of the above effects come into play. There is enhanced **readiness to move**, **enhanced attention** and **priority selection** of the expected stimulus. The athlete has already interpreted the meaning of the starting gun and knows what action must be taken before it goes off.

Factors which influence set come under two headings:

1. Aspects of the stimulus itself such as the context within which it occurs and any instructions which may have been given.
2. Aspects which relate to the individual. These include individual differences in personality or intelligence, past experience, motivation, emotional states and cultural factors.

Context and Expectation

An example of the influence of context in inducing set is the experiment of Bruner and Minturn (1955). Participants were shown sequences either of letters or of numbers, for example:

C D E F G H or
8 9 10 11 12

When presented with an ambiguous figure/number – 13 –, which could be either B or 13, those who had seen the sequence of letters tended to perceive it as B, while those who had seen the numbers perceived it as 13. The context in which it was seen produced expectation and induced a particular 'set'.

Another instance where past experience seems to have induced a particular 'set' is in the experiment by Bruner and Postman (1949). Participants were presented tachistoscopically (over a very short, measured durations of time) with playing cards with suit colours reversed, i.e. black hearts and diamonds, red clubs and spades. At very short exposures the cards were reported as being normal. However as the exposures became longer, it became not uncommon for them to report purple or brown hearts. The stored experience of seeing playing cards had somehow begun to blend with the immediate stimulus information before them.

Motivation and Set

There have been many studies of the effect of food deprivation upon perception. An example is that of Gilchrist and Nesberg (1952). Participants were deprived of food or water for varying periods. When they were shown pictures of objects relating to food or drink they perceived them as having enhanced brightness, and this brightness increased up to the point where they had been deprived for eight hours. After they were allowed to eat or drink as much as they wanted brightness returned to base levels.

A number of studies have shown the effect of other kinds of motivation upon the way in which things are perceived. Solley and Haigh (1958), for instance, asked children aged four to eight to draw pictures of Santa Claus during the month running up to Christmas. As Christmas approached, Santa became larger, nearer and more elaborate (a more decorated costume and a bigger bag of presents). After Christmas, Santa shrank and his present bag all but disappeared.

Emotion and Perceptual Defence

Perceptual defence could be regarded as an 'anti-set', that is a predisposition not to perceive something which may have unpleasant emotional overtones. The term was originally that of McGinnies (1949). In a classic study participants were presented with either neutral words (such as 'table' 'apple' 'chair') or taboo words (like 'whore' 'penis' 'bitch'). Each of these words were presented very briefly to begin with then for increasing lengths of time by means of a tachistoscope (a device which presents a very brief measured stimulus) until subjects were able to name them. This point was the recognition threshold. At the same time a measure of emotional response (Galvanic Skin Response or GSR) was taken. It was found that the taboo words had a higher recognition threshold and were also accompanied by greater GSR.

There were problems, though, with this. It was pointed out by Howes and Solomon (1951) that the taboo words were likely to be less familiar, and also that difference might reflect, not difference in perception, but differences in response. Bitterman and Kniffin (1953) and Aronfreed *et al.* (1953) provided evidence that participants might feel embarrassed to utter the taboo words and might delay until they were completely sure.

Worthington (1969) attempted to resolve the matter by presenting 160 participants with two spots of light and asking them to say which was brighter. In fact there was no difference in brightness, but embedded in each spot was a word too dim to be consciously perceived (i.e. subliminal). The words had previously been rated for emotional content. Those words with high emotional rating were consistently perceived as dimmer. This does seem to back up McGinnies' idea of perceptual defence. Hardy and Legge (1967) also found evidence to support the idea.

Values, Culture and Personality

There is some evidence that an individual's value system may induce a set. Postman *et al.* (1948) rated participants on the Allport-Vernon scale of values. This divides values into six categories:

Theoretical
Aesthetic
Social
Political
Economic
Religious

These categories represent the kind of things which individuals think are important. Words which related to highly rated value categories were found to be more easily perceived than lower-rated values.

Witkin *et al.* (1949) identified two different cognitive styles, which they labelled field-dependent and field-independent. These relate to different ways of perceiving which are linked to personality characteristics. They represent differences in the abilities of individuals to separate background (or field) from figure. This was measured by means of a Rod and Frame Test (RFT) or an Embedded Figures Test (EFT). In the RFT, a rod was shown inside a square frame, tilted away from the vertical. The participant's task was to adjust the rod so that it was vertical. Those who were field independent found this easier than field-dependent people who were more likely to line the rod up with the frame. You could argue that the latter had a perceptual set induced more easily by the context in which they saw things.

Cultural Set

In Pettigrew *et al.*'s (1958) study, different racial groups of South Africans were assembled (English and Afrikaans-speaking white people, Indians, Africans and people of mixed race). They were shown photographs by means of a binocular tachistoscope. Different pictures were presented to each of their two eyes, Pictures of a member of one race were shown to one eye, of another to the other simultaneously. Afrikaaners tended to exhibit a cultural set in that they saw all the pictures as either European or African without differentiating Indians and those of mixed race from the Africans. This seems to show evidence that their prejudices had had an effect upon their perception of the photographs. Their classification of everyone they encountered as either white or non-white was carried over into their perceptions.

From the above it can be seen that perceptions are influenced by a whole range of factors relating to the individual. These include cultural background and experience, personality, values, motivations (both extrinsic and intrinsic), the context in which something is perceived and the individual's expectations.

Self-assessment Questions

1. Make some comparison between:
    (a) Neisser's cyclic and Gregory's perceptual hypothesis theory of perception;
    (b) Brunswik's model and Gibson's theory of direct perception.
    In each case identify and comment on the differences and similarities.
2. List factors which contribute to the establishment of set. Which of them are external, which internal to the individual?
3. List the Gestalt principles of perceptual organisation. What evidence is there that these principles are not innate but learned through experience?

SECTION IV   VISUAL ILLUSIONS

As has been seen (p. 35) perception is a dynamic process of searching for the best available interpretation of the data received through the senses. It is not a passive reflection of sensations received, but an active process of testing hypotheses. Sometimes the data received is ambiguous, or at least the brain conceives it to be so, so that the interpretation is erroneous (an illusion), or vacillating (at one moment there is one perception, at the next another). The field of illusion is a wide one and this section will confine itself to a discussion of those visual illusions which contribute to an understanding of some of the issues discussed in Sections II and III.

Illusions which Distort Reality

Perhaps the most famous (and most studied) illusion is the arrowhead illusion, first described by Franz Müller-Lyer in 1889 (see Figure 3.13).

The explanation given by Gregory (1968) for the fact that the line between the outward pointing arrowheads (A–B) appears to be

FIGURE 3.13
The Müller-Lyer Illusion

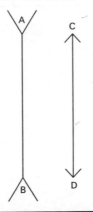

longer than that between the inward pointing ones (C–D) (though they are in fact the same length) relates to depth perception and size constancy. If you see A–B as the furthest corner of the inside of a room, then the arrowheads might represent the floor and the ceiling. These are nearer than the corner (A–B). You might see C–D on the other hand as the nearest corner of the outside of a building. The arrowheads then represent walls receding into the distance (see Figure 3.14).

Experience of the relationship between size and distance encourages the observer to perceive A–B as more distant (and so smaller) than C–D. Sensory data on the other hand, presents them as the same length. The brain, therefore, uses size constancy and scales up A–B to be longer than C–D.

A very similar effect is that of the Ponzo illusion first described by Mario Ponzo in 1913 (see Figure 3.15).

The line A–B in this illusion appears to be longer than C–D. If we imagine the outer lines as railway track receding into the distance, then linear perspective dictates that A–B must be further away than C–D and so should be shorter. But sensory data received shows the lines to be the same length. A–B is thus perceived as longer as a result of size constancy scaling.

FIGURE 3.14

An Explanation of the Müller-Lyer Illusion (after Gregory, 1968)

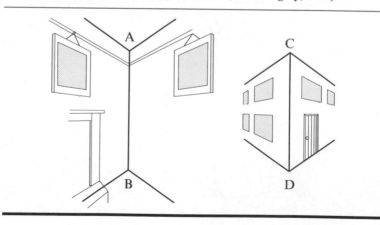

FIGURE 3.15

The Ponzo Illusion

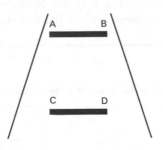

Gregory measured the extent of the illusion in each of these two cases by asking participants in his experiment to select a line which seemed to match lines at various positions between the converging outer lines (in the case of the Ponzo illusion) or else to adjust a light to match the apparent depth of each line, when pairs of lines were presented. In the case of the Müller-Lyer illusion, the arrow angles were varied from 40 degrees through to 170 degrees. The amount of the illusion varied from the line being perceived as nearly one centimeter shorter than reality at 40 degrees, to 1.5 cm longer at 150 degrees.

A Commentary on Gregory's Explanation

1. What Gregory is claiming is that the internal processes of interpreting what we see use the apparent distance as a gauge of size. In the cases of figures such as the Müller-Lyer arrowheads or Ponzo's converging tracks, size constancy is applied wrongly. But then the question might be asked: Why do these figures appear flat, if the effect they have is as though they were 3D? Gregory (1970) suggested this was because they were lying on a flat surface. When they were presented in the dark as luminous two-dimensional outlines, Gregory claimed that they were in fact seen in 3D. But this 3D image does not seem to be seen by everyone. Stacey and Pike

(1970) argued that instead of apparent distance determining the size, the size we see things determines the distance we think they are away from us.

2. Eysenck (1984) has noted that the Müller-Lyer illusion is still seen when circles or squares replace the fins (see Figure 3.16). This

FIGURE 3.16

Circles or Squares replace Arrowheads in the Müller-Lyer Illusion

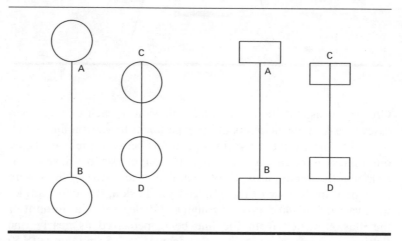

does not really fit with Gregory's explanation either. There is no size constancy scaling involved in this case. The difference in the apparent length may be related to whether it is seen as part of a large or a small object.

3. Day (1980) has suggested that more than one factor contributes to the Müller-Lyer illusion. The issue relates to whether what we perceive depends upon a detailed analysis of the information received through our senses (bottom-up processing) or whether it is primarily a matter of context and expectation (top-down processing).

4. Perhaps the factors which determine what we see include the conditions under which we view the figures. Gregory has tended to present the figures using a tachistoscope, which gives a brief

exposure under controlled and perhaps not optimal conditions. In these circumstances it is not perhaps surprising that context and expectations become important. Gibson (1972) on the other hand, as the main proponent of bottom-up processing, has tended to use optimal viewing conditions.

Context and Illusion

The circles illusion (Figure 3.17) illustrates well the effect of **context** upon perception.

FIGURE 3.17

The Circles Illusion (Circle A is the same size as Circle B)

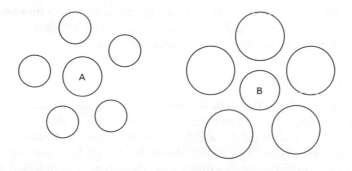

The context of the outer circles, larger in one case, smaller in the other, leads us to exaggerate the size of the centre circle in A and reduce the size of the centre circle in B.

In all these cases we have misinterpreted the data available to our brains, which comes either from the senses directly, or from experiences of similar sensory experiences in the past stored in memory.

Illusions Resulting in Ambiguous Figures

The Necker cube (see Figure 3.18) is a good illustration of an ambiguous figure. The data is insufficient to enable us to make an

FIGURE 3.18
The Necker Cube

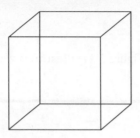

unambiguous interpretation of what our senses tell us, so that what is perceived seems to vacillate. At one moment we are looking down on a cube, at another up into it (Necker, 1832).

Paradoxical Figures

Sometimes interpretation of the sensory data results in perceptions of impossible figures. The cues to depth perception pp. 41–4 have been deliberately used by artists to provide false and impossible perceptions. Figure 3.19 shows Hogarth's use of false perspective in 1754 to provide an impossible scene. There is no way in which the man on the distant hill could light his pipe from the candle held by the woman leaning out of her upstairs window. It is an interesting exercise to count the instances in the picture where false depth cues have led to impossible perceptions.

Figure Ground Illusions

One of the most commonly-found sets of illusions which either provide ambiguity or error in perception relate to **figure and background**. One of the organising processes which has been discussed pp. 54–6 under the heading of 'Gestalt perceptual organisation' is the distinction between figure and ground. Whenever a set of images is presented, it is necessary to distinguish what

FIGURE 3.19

False Perspective

Reproduced with permission from E. H. Gombrich, *Art and Illusion* (Oxford: Phaidon Press, 1960) p. 205. The illustration was originally published as a frontispiece to *Dr Brook Taylor's Method of Perspective Made Easy*, by John Joshua Kirby, London, 1754.

parts form the main focus of the images and what constitutes the background or context. Look at a picture of cows grazing in a field and immediately the image will be organised in your mind as figure (the cows) and ground (the field and surrounding landscape). Well-known illusions occur when this organisation becomes difficult. Examples include the Rubin vase (Figure 3.20).

FIGURE 3.20

The Rubin Vase

The observer sees alternately either a vase or two faces in profile looking at each other (Rubin, 1915).

Processing Strategies

Much of what has been discussed in this section has related to what Coren and Girgus (1978) refer to as **processing strategies**, that is to say decisions taken by the brain about the data presented to it, in the light of such things as learning, past experience, motivations and expectations. A further explanation for some illusory effects are referred to by Coren and Girgus as **structural effects**. These are the result of the biological and optical construction of the eye. For example, the retina is not flat but concave, so that there is some distortion. Try this:

Exercise

Cut a long strip of paper about 2.5 cms wide and 50 cms long. Make a mark in the centre and focus upon it. What do you notice about the edges of the paper at the extreme ends?

You should become aware of the barrel illusion. The paper will no longer appear parallel at the ends, but will bend inwards.

With some illusions (for example the Poggendorf illusion, Figure 3.21) the visual effects are due partly to processing strategies, partly to structural effects (Poggendorf, 1860). Coren and Girgus (1972) showed that after five minutes of looking at the illusion it had decreased by 39 per cent. Processing strategies adapt after a period so that it is evident that 39 per cent represents the proportion of the illusion due to these strategies, while the remainder might be attributed to structural effects (optical features and neural effects in the retina and in the brain). This again relates to the debate concerning bottom-up or top-down processing in perception.

The diagonal lines do in fact intersect the two vertical lines, though the left line appears higher than the right. Test this by putting a straight edge along the lines.

FIGURE 3.21

The Poggendorf Illusion

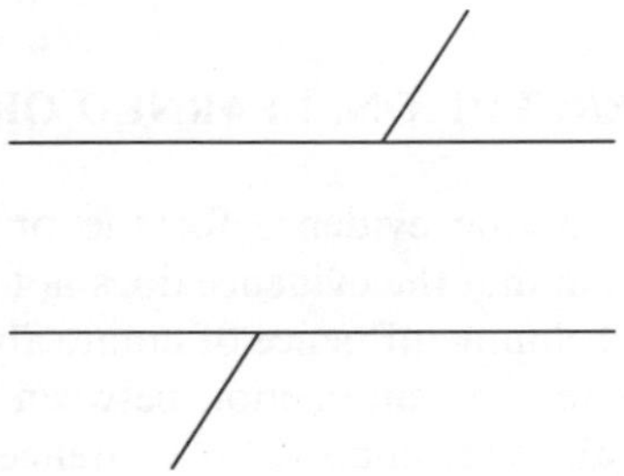

An Overview of Visual Illusions and Explanations for Them

Visual illusions represent cases where the information presented to the brain through the senses is either incorrectly or ambiguously interpreted. There seem to be two explanations which can be offered for this.

1. A top-down processing explanation which emphasises the ambiguity of the cues which help with interpretation. Factors involved here include: (a) the context in which the illusion is seen (the circles illusion illustrates this); and (b) expectations resulting from past experience (Gregory's explanation for Müller-Lyer and Ponzo depend upon this and upon size constancy and depth cues).
2. Structural explanations, which include optical features of what is seen and neural effects on the retina and in the brain. These can be said to be bottom-up processing explanations. The work of Coren and Girgus mentioned above illustrates this.

Self-assessment Questions

1. Describe some explanations of visual illusions relating to processing strategies and show how illusions such as Müller-Lyer and Ponzo can be explained.
2. What is the role of experience in the perception of illusions?
3. Describe the ways in which top-down and bottom-up processing strategies have been brought in to explain illusions.
4. How do figure ground illusions such as the Rubin vase relate to Gestalt theories of perception?

SECTION V   PERCEPTION, LEARNED OR INNATE?

This section sets out the evidence for the origins of perceptual ability. It will be seen that the evidence does not point clearly either towards the overwhelming influence of innate ability or of learning, but rather that there is an interaction between innate endowment and environmental experience. The evidence comes from the following sources:

1. **Neonate studies**. These are studies using either new-born humans or animals. They show perceptual ability even in newly born creatures.
2. **Deprivation studies.** Deprivation studies are those which examine, either with humans or with animals, the effects upon perception of deprivation of sensation, particularly sight and distortion of vision.

Neonate Studies

Evidence from human neonates is often hard to interpret, as it has to be inferred from their reactions to stimuli placed before them. This inference is sometimes subjective.

Fantz (1961) showed that babies were able to distinguish patterns, suggesting the possibility that figure/ground discrimination as well as some kind of form perception might be innate or at the least learned very early in life.

The babies were placed in a specially-designed **looking chamber**, which enabled observers to measure the time the babies spent looking at cards with various patterns. Figure 3.22 shows some of the images presented to babies in Fantz's experiments. Results included the following:

1. Babies as young as two days old spent longer looking at patterned cards than at plain grey ones.
2. Striped bullseye or checkerboard patterns were preferred to plain squares or discs.
3. Infants from four days to 6 months old preferred face-like patterns, even scrambled faces, to unpatterned stimuli containing the same amount of light and dark.

Fantz came to the conclusion that babies' preference for face-like patterns was innate. Moreover, the preference for face-like images was linked with their social needs. They clearly had a need to identify their caregivers. Some limitations of the study include:

FIGURE 3.22

Some Images from Fantz's Experiments

1. The possibility that preference for the scrambled against the unscrambled face was because the former was asymmetrical. Studies with non-face patterns had shown a preference for symmetrical over asymmetrical patterns.
2. The preference technique adopted has limitations. It is better at showing what the babies like to look at than what they are able to discriminate.

Maurer and Barrera (1981) used both Fantz's **preference** technique and also a **habituation** technique. Instead of measuring preferences as between pairs of stimuli (as Fantz had done) they presented one stimulus at a time and measured the time the babies fixated it before looking away. They did this repeatedly until the child was bored with it and looked away after a very short time. Then an unhabituated image was presented. If the fixation time returned to what it had been initially, the babies clearly were able to discriminate between the two images. Stimuli included 'natural' faces, scrambled but symmetrical faces, and asymmetrical ones (see Figure 3.23). At one month old there was no significant difference in fixation times between any of the stimuli. At two months, however, there was a significant preference for a natural face.

FIGURE 3.23

Stimuli used by Maurer and Barrera (1981)

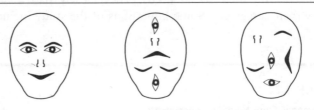

Maurer and Barrera's research seems to show that figure/ground discrimination is either learned within the first month of a baby's life or else that it is a matter of **maturation**, that is to say, it is a matter of normal development, independent of external stimulation. Some doubt is thrown on Fantz's conclusions.

The researchers also showed a development within infant perception. By two months old, babies were taking an interest in facial features (Maurer, 1983). By three to six months, they were discriminating between different facial patterns, between a smiling and a frowning face, for instance (Barrera and Maurer, 1981). Samuels and Ewy (1985) found that by the same age they could discriminate between attractive and unattractive faces.

Depth Perception and Size Constancy

Bower *et al.* (1970) investigated responses of very young babies (6 to 20 days old) to a cube which loomed towards their faces. As it came close, they made defensive movements, such as throwing up their arms, moving their heads back or opening their eyes very wide. However, later studies such as that of Yonas (1981) only succeeded in establishing an eye-blink response to looming stimuli in infants of one month old. Accurate depth-perception is indicated by the ability of babies to reach out and grasp objects which they can see and this ability is not achieved until about six months. However, Harris (1983) showed that there was some evidence of adjustment to distance by about three-and-a-half to four-and-a-half months.

In their classic experiment Gibson and Walk (1960) used a **visual cliff**, illustrated in Figure 3.24 overleaf. At one side of the central path the checkerboard pattern is covered by glass immediately above it; on the other there is an apparent drop with the checkerboard pattern several feet below the glass.

The researchers showed that six-month-old babies were reluctant to crawl over the 'cliff', even when their mothers encouraged them to do so. Of course, babies old enough to crawl have already had time to learn to perceive depth, but the researchers also used newly born (or hatched) animals. Some, such as newly hatched chicks, are fully mobile almost as soon as they are hatched. Even as young as 24 hours old, chicks invariably hopped off on the 'shallow' side of the central runway and refused to move on to the 'deep' side. Similarly, kids and lambs (which can walk almost as soon as they are born), always stepped on to the shallow, never on to the deep side, indicating that they can perceive depth.

Bower's (1965) experiments with size constancy are also interesting in this context. Bower reinforced a head turning response in babies from 40 to 60 days old by a peek-a-boo response from an

FIGURE 3.24
Gibson and Walk's 'Visual Cliff' (1960)

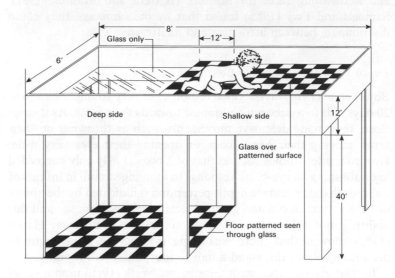

adult. When this response was established, Bower only reinforced the babies when head-turning occurred in the presence of a 30 cm cube one metre away. Bower then presented four stimuli in counterbalanced order:

1. the original 30 cm cube at one metre distant;
2. the 30 cm cube at three metres distant;
3. a 90 cm cube one metre away; and
4. a 90 cm cube three metres away.

The prediction was that if the babies did not have size constancy they would respond equally to (1) and to (4) (the retinal size was the same in both cases). If the babies had size constancy, they should respond to (2), (the same object) or to (3), (the same distance away). In the event there were 98 responses to (1), only 22 to (4) while (2) and (3) elicited 58 and 54 responses respectively. This indicated that at that age babies have some appreciation of size constancy. While this does not conclusively show perception to be innate, it shows that certain facets of it are at the least learned very early.

Deprivation and Readjustment Studies

These studies include:

1. Those which set out to deprive animals of early perceptual learning.
2. Studies of humans, deprived of sight from birth, who have had their sight restored later in life.
3. Studies with humans using distorting glasses.

Animal studies

In Riesen's (1950) experiments chimpanzees were deprived of light for the first sixteen months of their lives (except for several 45-second intervals of light each day for feeding). When they were tested at sixteen months old, they showed normal pupil constriction to light, but did not blink when threatening movements were made to their faces and showed no interest in their toys except through touch. However, Weiskrantz (1956) found that these visual problems were the result of poor development of the retina because of light deprivation. Another chimpanzee reared by Riesen in a translucent mask to mitigate this also showed poor visual ability. The suggestion was that not only light but also patterned visual images are necessary for the proper development of sight.

Similar research by Hubel and Wiesel (1962) found incomplete development of receptive fields after kittens had been reared with full or partial blindfolds. Blakemore and Cooper (1966) reared kittens in a large drum which allowed them to see only vertical stripes. When they were tested it was found that they responded to vertical, but not to horizontal lines. These experiments only show that proper development of physiological vision is dependent upon experience, not that perception (in the sense of the interpretation of what is presented to the senses) is innate.

Studies Using Human Participants

Gregory and Wallace (1963) describe in some detail the case of a man (S.B.) who received a corneal graft at the age of 52 after having been blind from birth. While he made very good progress after the bandages were removed from his eyes and he was able to see, he had problems with things which he had not previously been able to touch. Where he was familiar with objects from touch his judgements of size and distance were good. However, he became depressed with the drabness of the world around him, gradually gave up active living and died three years later. There was clearly deep emotional disturbance.

This study does seem to show that S.B. depended upon the learning of touch perception which he had had to employ while he was blind and found it hard to learn to perceive visually, separately from this. It provides some evidence for the necessity of learning in perception, but again by no means conclusive evidence. Other evidence regarding blind people who have regained their sight in adulthood comes from the work of Von Senden, whose account of 65 such cases was analysed by Hebb (1949). His analysis included an assessment of:

1. Their ability to detect a figure or an object (Hebb terms this **figural unity**).
2. Their ability to name or identify the object (Hebb refers to this as **figural identity**).

He came to the conclusion that figural unity was innate, while figural identity had to be learned. These people seemed to be able to discriminate figure from background right away. Objects which were familiar to them from touch, however, and this includes faces, could not be identified by sight alone. They also showed little evidence of perceptual constancy (see pp. 45–8). There are some problems related to these studies, however, which include the following:

1. Adults will have learned about the world through their senses. Loss of a sense modality is compensated for to some extent by the other senses. There is, therefore, a certain amount of unlearning needed of existing ways of experiencing the world.

There will be a tendency for them to stick with what they know.

2. A radical alteration in someone's life (by having a new world of vision opened up, for instance) has emotional consequences for which there may have been little preparation. The depression Gregory's patient, S.B. exhibited seems to have been common in Von Senden's cases.
3. The years of blindness may have resulted in a deterioration of the visual system. It may be this, rather than the need for learning which accounted for the problems encountered.
4. Von Senden's cases date from 1700 to 1928. The reliability of some of them, at least, may be suspect.

Studies Using Distorting Glasses

There are a number of studies involving the distortion of normal vision which provide some evidence for perceptual learning. Stratton (1897) wore an inverting lens on one eye (with the other one covered) for a period of eight days. He reported that he noticed the inversion less and less as the days went by. He could get around the house without bumping into things by the fifth day and his surroundings looked normal enough while he was moving about, but when he stopped and concentrated on what was about him things still seemed upside-down. When the inverting lens was removed he found the environment bewildering to some extent, but not upside-down. It is open to question whether it was his perception which had adjusted to the glasses or whether it was his body movements.

There have been many attempts to repeat Stratton's experiment. Ewert (1930) made participants in his experiment wear binocular inverting lenses for between 175 and 195 hours. He aimed to see whether perceptual adaptation did occur or whether the participants simply learnt to cope better. Two tests were administered on each day of the experiment:

1. Coloured blocks were presented to each participant in a line from an observation point. Participants had to name the colours of the nearest and the farthest blocks. Up and down and left and right judgements remained inverted throughout the experiment. There was no sign of adaptation.

2. He tested for motor adaptation and found progressive improvement in ability to locate things by touch. This seems to be improved coping ability rather than perceptual adaptation.

Kohler (1964) used an optical device with a mirror which inverted the image vertically but not left to right. In his experiment, which lasted ten days, he found that the participants were able to see things the right way up provided that they moved about and touched objects in his environment. The more familiar objects became, the greater the likelihood that they would be seen upright. Moreover, when the inverting apparatus was finally removed objects were sometimes seen to be upside down, though only briefly.

If there seems to be a contradiction between the findings of Kohler and those of Ewert several factors should be remembered:

1. The apparatus was different. Kohler's apparatus inverted vertically only, not left and right.
2. Participants in Ewert's experiments were just given particular tests to carry out, whereas Kohler's had to practise a wide variety of perceptual-motor tasks, moving around the laboratory and picking things up.
3. The number of participants was not very great (nine in all). There were likely to be considerable differences between the individuals in their reactions to what they were being asked to do. It is therefore very difficult to make any generalisation.

The evidence provided by these studies seems to support the view that there is a strong element of learning in perception. If, for instance, participants in Stratton's, Kohler's or Ewert's studies found that when their vision was distorted in some way they were able gradually to adapt to the distortion, this adaptation seems to be a process of learning to come to terms with the new visual circumstance. Similarly, where individuals have regained their sight (as in the case of Gregory's S.B.) and found that they could not immediately see perfectly there was a necessity for some unlearning of established patterns of perception (using other sense modalities than sight). This suggests that both the original mode of perception as well as the new one have had to be learned.

Cross-Cultural Studies

Cross-cultural studies also provide some evidence for the effects of different perceptual environments on the way in which individuals perceive the world. Several of these studies involve the presentation of illusions (such as those discussed in Section IV of this chapter) to people with a different cultural background. Illusions such as the Müller-Lyer or Ponzo illusions seem to depend upon the **carpentered nature** of the environment in which most Western people live. There is a preponderance of straight lines which may be viewed from different angles. The explanation given by Gregory (1968) depends upon linear perspective as it is seen in a world of predominantly straight lines.

Segall *et al.* (1966) re-examined a finding by Rivers early this century (1901) that while non-Westernised people in Papua New Guinea were less susceptible to the Müller-Lyer (M-L) illusion, they were more susceptible to the Horizontal-Vertical (H-V) illusion (see Figure 3.25) than English people. They suggested that while the M-L illusion depends upon the prevalence of right angles in the environment (a carpentered environment) the foreshortening of lines which fall on the retina vertically (the horizontal-vertical illusion) depends in part upon where people

---

FIGURE 3.25

The Horizontal-Vertical Illusion (distance from A to B is the same as from B to C)

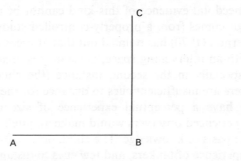

live. People living mostly outdoors in open, spacious environments would be more susceptible to it. Rain forest dwellers on the other hand would be less susceptible. Segall *et al.* had M-L and H-V illusions presented to people in thirteen different African countries and the findings largely supported their hypotheses. There have been criticisms of this study, though, which include the following:

1. Segall *et al.* did not consider the effects of Western education and other cultural variables. Jahoda (1966) has suggested that these might be very important.
2. Susceptibility to M-L decreases with age. If there is an impact by the environment on perceptual development it must occur at an early age. It is quite possible that the individuals tested spent their early years in quite a different environment (Weaver, 1974).

Size constancy also seems to be dependent on experience. Cole and Scribner (1974) report anecdotal evidence derived from Turnbull's (1961) study of pygmies in the Iturbi forest in West Africa. These were forest dwellers whose experience of perception at a distance was limited. A pygmy accompanied Turnbull out of the forest and saw cows grazing at a distance. Though the pygmy knew what cows were, he nevertheless thought he was looking at ants! Turnbull also reports that a Kpelle child raised in the jungle but taken to the capital city of Monrovia saw large tanker ships far out at sea from a high window of a hotel on a hill top. The child commented on the bravery of people who would go out to sea in such small boats.

There are problems, with this kind of evidence, though:

- Anecdotal evidence of this kind cannot be as valid as evidence that comes from a properly-controlled study.
- Vernon (1970) has pointed out that at great distances, especially with an intervening space, constancy is greatly reduced.
- Especially in the second instance (the child and the tankers) there are insufficient cues to distance for the observer to be able to have a perceptual experience of size constancy. Instead, experienced observers would make an intellectual judgement on the basis of knowledge. The child, on the other hand, having no experience of tankers, and few cues to distance would have little to go on to make a correct judgement of size.

Conclusion

It is not possible to arrive at a definitive conclusion about the origins of perception. Some aspects, such as size constancy and figure-ground discrimination seem (from the neonate studies of Bower and Fantz, for instance) to be present in very young children. Children and young animals also seem to be able to perceive depth very young, as has been shown in Walk and Gibson's experiments. What perceptual abilities are innate is much harder to prove. Maturation (the natural development of a baby independently of its environment) might go some way towards providing an explanation, but perhaps a more likely conclusion is that there are innate perceptual schemata which provide a basis for interaction with the environment and the development of other perceptual skills.

Distortion and deprivation studies also seem to be inconclusive. It is hard to compare human perception with that of chimpanzees or kittens, and in any case deficiencies in perceptual abilities in studies of young animals seem to be due more to deficient physiological development than to deficient psychological learning. The number of participants in studies such as those of Stratton, Ewert and Kohler does not allow generalisation. There might well be individual differences among them sufficient to confound any overall effect. Gregory's and Von Senden's studies are also inconclusive, though there are indications that the sense-modality which has dominated an individual's life has a permanent and profound bearing on how he or she perceives the world when circumstances have altered. It does, therefore, provide some evidence for the influence of learning. Cross-cultural studies perhaps also provide evidence for learning. Where environmental conditions have been different, what is perceived is different (susceptibility to visual illusions, for instance).

Self-assessment Questions

1. What evidence does the work of Fantz provide that perception is innate? Do you find it convincing?
2. Deprivation studies with animals provide some evidence for perception being learned. Does it seem satisfactory to you?
3. What evidence can be gained from cross-cultural studies that perception is learned?

FURTHER READING

N. J. Wade and M. Swanston, *Visual Perception* (London: Routledge, 1991).

R. L. Gregory, *Eye and Brain*, 3rd edition (London: Weidenfeld and Nicolson, 1977).

R. Serpell (for cross-cultural studies of perception), *Culture's Influence on Behaviour* (London: Methuen, 1970).

P. K. Smith and H. Cowie (for the nature/nurture of perception), *Understanding Children's Development* (Oxford: Blackwell, 1988).

Memory Processes 4

At the end of this chapter you should be able to:

1. Describe some of the early attempts to examine human memory, including research by Ebbinghaus and Bartlett.
2. Make an evaluation of the merits of 'the modal' model of memory.
3. Identify what is meant by iconic and echoic memory and its relationship with short term and long term memory.
4. Describe and evaluate alternatives to the modal model of memory including 'levels of processing' and 'working memory' models.
5. Distinguish between episodic and semantic memory.
6. Describe some of the research into ways in which long-term memory is organised.
7. Identify ways in which memory research has been made more relevant to 'real life', including research into autobiographical memory, prospective memory and eyewitness testimony.
8. Apply techniques practically which are aimed at improving your own memory, with an understanding of their basis in research.

INTRODUCTION

This chapter examines the processes involved in the storage and retrieval of information. These include:

1. The processes which enable human beings to store information just long enough to be able to use it (this might be termed either **short term** or **working memory**).
2. The storage of information for use in the longer term (**long term memory**).
3. The ways in which material is **organised for storage** and processes of retrieval from the long term store.

4. Some of the ways in which memory research has been conducted outside laboratories (ecologically valid, or 'real life' memory research).
5. Techniques and strategies for making the best use of memory.

SECTION I   EARLY RESEARCH INTO MEMORY

1. Ebbinghaus and the Associationist approach

Ebbinghaus (1885) approached the subject of memory from an **associationist** standpoint. This was in the tradition of the empiricists of the 17th and 18th centuries, particularly Locke, Berkeley and Hume. When experiences occur together they will tend to be associated and so remembered together. Ebbinghaus used rigorously-controlled experiments to explore the ways in which associations were formed and stored. Because of the importance of association, familiar and meaningful words could not be used as stimulus material. It was impossible to know how such words would fit into the existing web of a person's ideas. Ebbinghaus, therefore, created and used nonsense syllables, consisting of a consonant followed by a vowel followed by another consonant (**consonant-vowel-consonant trigrams or** CVCs), which he generated in hundreds and used as the material to be remembered. The associations formed between these CVCs were (theoretically, at any rate) entirely new ones unaffected by the individual's previous experience. His experiments were as carefully controlled as possible. He researched memory using himself as his own subject, varying systematically the number of times he read a list of CVCs over to himself, and the delay between reading the lists and recalling them.

Some Results of Ebbinghaus's Experiments

In one series of experiments he varied (between 20 minutes and a month) the delay between an initial learning of a list of CVCs and relearning them to the same standard of retention. Then he measured the number of relearning trials which were needed at each delay interval. As might be expected the greater the delay, the more relearning trials were required. Forgetting was found to be very rapid at first, slowing down as the delay increased.

The contribution which Ebbinghaus made to memory research lay in the development of a methodology of laboratory research; the use of nonsense syllables to control the effects of meaning; the use of free recall (recall in any order) or serial recall (recall of learned material in the order in which it was presented); and systematic manipulation of variables. Many of the methods he employed have been used in later research.

On the other hand it could be said that he encouraged researchers to concentrate upon recall of meaningless nonsense syllables rather than upon more ecologically valid research.

2. A Constructivist Approach

The **constructivist** approach focuses on meaningful material and more natural situations rather than lists of CVCs. Bartlett (1932) provided participants in his studies with stories to remember. A well-known one, entitled 'The War of the Ghosts' is reproduced below:

> One night two young men from Egulac went down to the river to hunt seals, and while they were there it became foggy and calm. Then they heard war-cries, and they thought, 'Maybe this is a war-party'. They escaped to the shore, and hid behind a log. Now canoes came up, and they heard the noise of paddles, and saw one canoe coming up to them. There were five men in the canoe, and they said, 'What do you think? We will take you along. We are going up the river to make war on the people.'
>
> One of the young men said, 'I have no arrows.' 'Arrows are in the canoe', they said. 'I will not go along. I might be killed. My relatives do not know where I have gone. But you,' he said, turning to the other, 'may go with them.' So one of the young men went, the other returned home. And the warriors went on up the river to a town on the other side of Kalama. The people came down to the water, and they began to fight, and many were killed. But presently the young man heard one of the warriors say, 'Quick, let us go home; that Indian has been hit.' Now he thought, 'Oh, they are ghosts.' He did not feel sick, but they said he had been shot.
>
> So the canoes went back to Egulac, and the young man went ashore to his house and made a fire. And he told everybody and

said, 'Behold, I accompanied the ghosts, and we went to fight. Many of our fellows were killed and many of those who attacked us were killed. They said I was hit but I did not feel sick.'

He told it all and then became quiet. When the sun rose he fell down. Something black came out of his mouth. His face became contorted. The people jumped up and cried. He was dead. (Bartlett, 1932, p. 65)

Participants had to study stories like the above for 15 minutes and then recall as much of it as they could. Comparisons were then made between the participants' versions and the original. Recalled versions tended to be shorter and contained distortions. Memory for the story was tested several times with different intervals of time between the study of the story and the recall. The longest interval was ten years. Changes in the recalled version embraced the following categories:

1. *Omission*: detail tended to be omitted which did not fit in with the way in which the individual had conceived the story.
2. *Rationalisation*: new material was sometimes brought in to make the story more logical.
3. *Emphasis*: the importance given in the story to particular aspects was sometimes altered. A theme (the ghost idea, for instance) might be made more central than it had been in the original.
4. *Order*: the order of events was sometimes transformed.
5. *Distortions*: individuals constructed their recall from their own attitudes, cultural background and their own emptional reaction to the story which in turn reflected their individual experiences in life.

Bartlett did not just use stories to illustrate how memory tended towards an active reconstruction of recalled events rather than a passive, almost photograhic, reproduction of them. Participants in his experiments studied memory for faces, line drawings and ink blots. The most important determinants of human memory (in Bartlett's view) were the individuals' effort to find meaning in the context of their experience. Where the meaning in something which a person is asked to recall is obscure, then meaning is re-created. Perhaps this constructivist view of memory might be compared with Gregory's view of perception as an active effort on the part of the perceiver to interpret the data coming to a person's senses in a way which has meaning.

Self-assessment Questions

1. What were the differences between the associationist and constructivist approaches to the study of memory?
2. List some of the changes which Bartlett found when his stories were recalled.

SECTION II SOME MODELS OF MEMORY

This section will discuss some of the later approaches which have been adopted for the study of memory. These range from two or three process memory models which envisaged separate stores, a **sensory buffer or visual information store (VIS)**, a **short-term store (STS)** and a **long-term store**, to the **depth of processing approach** of Craik and Lockhart (1972) and the **working memory** approach adopted by Baddeley and his colleagues (Baddeley and Hitch, 1974).

More Recent Approaches to Memory

There have been three strands of development in later studies of memory:

1. In much the same way that research into selective attention has concentrated upon models, memory researchers have produced flow-charts to illustrate the stages by which bits of information are processed. This might be described as an **information processing** approach. It is essentially **bottom up**. That is to say it concentrates upon the capacity of memory at each stage and on the length of time material might remain in a particular stage. It does not take much account of the individual or of the context within which the memory occurs.
2. A second approach makes a more **top down** interpretation of memory. Individuals come into a memory situation with their own intentions, mental abilities and experience. The **cognitive approach**, as it can be termed, takes this context into account.

3. What might be called an **ecological approach** to the study of memory has begun to be developed since the 1970s. As a result of Neisser's (1976) criticisms of much of the traditional laboratory-based research into memory, more emphasis has been placed on how memory functions in everyday life. This tends to be a more functional approach concentrating upon memory for faces, names, birthdays and appointments rather than for nonsense syllables or line drawings.

Information Processing Models of Memory

The model of memory which underpins much of modern research concentrates upon three memory stages:

1. A **learning or input stage**, which deals with the way in which information enters the memory system – and, of course, the factors which are likely to make this process easier or more difficult.
2. A **storage stage**, concerned with how information is organised within the memory system in order to be retained.
3. A **retrieval stage**, concerned with the processes involved in retrieving information from the memory for use.

A Modal Model of Memory

This **modal model** contains features of a number of similar models, including that of Atkinson and Shiffrin (1968). It envisages separate immediate, short-term and long-term memory storage stages. Information flows through the system with recoding operating at each stage. This is designed to show how information is acquired, stored and retrieved.

A distinction is made between three kinds of memory:

1. Immediate memory, which amounts to little more than a prolongation of the sensory stimulus, as it is received. Sperling (1960) called this the **Visual Information Store (VIS)**. Alternatively it has been called **iconic memory** (Neisser, 1967). A parallel process for the auditory modality has been called by Neisser an **echoic store**.

2. Short-term store (STS), which relates to the ability to retain information just long enough to use it. Typically it is the memory involved in retaining a telephone number just long enough to dial it after looking it up in a directory.
3. Long-term store (LTS) which relates to the ability to retain information over almost indefinite periods of time.

Figure 4.1 shows a flow diagram of the modal model of memory.
It is useful at this stage to examine a little more closely each of these stores.

FIGURE 4.1

Flow Diagram Illustrating the Modal Model of Memory

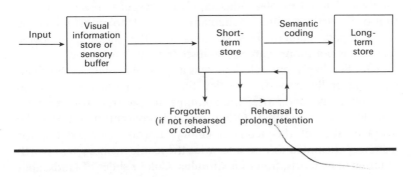

Immediate or Sensory Memory

Sperling (1960) developed what was termed the partial report technique, to establish the existence of the visual information store. Participants were presented with an array of three lines of four letters such as:

N R T V

W Y D A

P L H U

This array was presented to them for 50 milliseconds. At first, (in the **whole report method**) participants had to report all they had seen.

Participants were typically unable to report more than four out of twelve letters. Because Sperling did not believe that this represented a true picture of immediate recall, the **partial report method** was devised. Immediately after the array had been presented participants heard a tone: high, middle or low indicating that they were to report top, middle or lowest lines respectively. Clearly they had no chance, before the array was presented, to concentrate on any one line. The assumption was that they would have been able to report an equal proportion of whichever line they had been asked to report. Thus, if a participant was asked (by means of the tone) to report, say, the top line and reported N T V it was assumed that three letters could have been reported in each of the three lines, nine in all as opposed to the four letters achieved in the whole report method.

By varying the delay between the presentation of the array and the tone to indicate which line was to be reported Sperling was able to make an estimate of the duration of the iconic memory. If the tone was delayed by 500 milliseconds the response reverted to the four or five letters, which participants were able to report under the whole report method. This suggests that the duration of iconic memory is not more than 500 milliseconds (half a second).

After Sperling's research there was a spate of activity in this field, which generally supported the view that the icon lasted between 200 and 400 milliseconds after the stimulus disappeared, for example, van der Heijden (1981). Other research concentrated upon the characteristics of this iconic memory. Loftus *et al.* (1985), for instance, attempted to estimate what the iconic memory was worth in terms of memorisation of a stimulus. Colour slides of landscapes were presented for durations varying from 62 to 1300 milliseconds. There were three conditions:

1. A 'mask' condition where the presentation of the stimulus was immediately followed by a second slide showing a jumble of black and grey lines on a white background to prevent the formation of an icon.
2. A 'delayed mask' condition where there was an interval between the landscape slide and the mask.
3. A 'no mask' condition.

To test recall, the 72 landscape pictures together with 72 other slides, not previously seen, were shown and participants asked to indicate whether each slide was old or new. Participants' accuracy rates were interesting. For instance, where there was immediate masking it took 370 milliseconds exposure of the original slide to achieve the same accuracy (69 per cent) which had been achieved without masking with a 270 millisecond exposure. It might be said that iconic memory was worth 100 milliseconds exposure time.

However, Haber (1983a, 1983b, 1985) questioned the usefulness of iconic memory. His contention was that laboratory studies do not reflect what people do most of the time in real life. Most perception is of three-dimensional scenes and most involve movement. We are not often involved in trying to see things in brief flashes of light. However, it was pointed out that phenomena such as cinema films involve the integration into a moving whole of a series of brief light flashes. **Ecological validity**, while it is an important factor, needs to be balanced against scientific control of variables.

Echoic Memory

Echoic memory is a term coined by Neisser to be the auditory equivalent of iconic memory. It amounts to a brief continuation of auditory stimulation after the actual sound has stopped. This was tested by Darwin, Turvey and Crowder (1972). They presented participants with an auditory display and indicated to them which part of it was to be reported by means of a visual signal. The reverse, in fact, of Sperling's procedure. Special headphones presented three groups of items – digits and letters – one to the right ear; one to the left ear; the third recorded on both right and left channels so that it seemed to come from in-between the other two. Then participants were given a visual cue as to which of the three sequences of letters and numbers they should report. Results were similar to those of Sperling except that the capacity of echoic memory seemed to be about five items, as against nine for iconic memory. There might have been some difficulty for the participants in separating the three input channels. The duration, too, was different, 2 seconds approximately, as opposed to half a second for the iconic memory.

Duration of Echoic Memory

The duration of echoic memory was measured in an experiment by Crowder (1982). Participants heard two artificially-produced vowel sounds one after the other. Sometimes the vowel sounds were identical, sometimes merely similar. There were gaps between the presentations which ranged from 0.5 to 5 seconds. Participants had to report whether the vowel sounds were the same or not. An index of **discrimination ability** was produced which showed how accurately people were able to report whether the two sounds were different. Performance was most accurate at intervals of less than a second and accuracy deteriorated as the interval increased up to about three seconds, after which there was no change. Crowder surmised from this that the limit of duration of echoic memory seemed to be about three seconds. This was not very different from Darwin's estimate of two seconds.

Neuroscientific Evidence for Echoic Memory

Naatanen (1986) has summarised several pieces of research using **evoked cortical responses (ECR)**. There was mention of this technique in Chapter 2 Section IV (p. 32). Participants were told to concentrate on reading a book. While they were doing this, a tone of a specified frequency was repeatedly presented to them. On some trials this frequency was slightly different. Researchers found that there was a change in wave pattern about 200 milliseconds after the different tone was presented. This possibly indicates a duration of echoic memory of this length. Cowan (1984) has suggested that there might be two kinds of echoic storage, a short auditory storage of less than a second and a long auditory storage of several seconds duration. During the latter there might be some partial analysis and transformation of material. This might particularly apply to the spoken word, which needed to remain longer in storage to pick up additional cues coming later in a sentence.

Short-term Memory

The original proposal in the modal model, described above, was that Short Term Memory (STM) contained material which needed to be kept in store for not longer than 30 seconds as opposed to Long Term Memory (LTM), which was a more durable permanent store.

Memory Span

Once material has been selected by means of the immediate memory processes (the iconic or echoic memories) the model proposes that it passes into STM. Miller (1956) has suggested that the capacity of this store is limited to seven, plus or minus two items. In order to identify what this means in practice, conduct a brief test to identify your own memory span:

Exercise

Get a friend to present to you a series of digits (about one a second). Start with three numbers. When they have been presented, immediately repeat them in the correct order. Then proceed to four, then five numbers and so on. You memory span will be that number of digits which you can correctly repeat on 50 per cent of attempts.

Most people find that their memory span for digits is somewhere between five and nine (that is, seven plus or minus two). This holds good for groups or 'chunks' of numbers, letters or even larger units of information like words or phrases. Thus, while it is possible to recall only about eight or nine unrelated digits, it is not too hard to recall a London telephone number, e.g. 071 234 5498. These ten digits would normally be beyond most people's span but because they are grouped, the number is little more difficult to recall than three items would be.

Duration of STM

Unless it is possible to rehearse material to be recalled (that is, to keep repeating it silently or out loud) it will very quickly be forgotten. Peterson and Peterson (1959) did some experiments to test the duration of STM, using a technique which has become known as the **Brown-Peterson Technique**.

Participants were given groups of three consonants to recall. This should be well within their memory span. They were asked to repeat the consonants after intervals of 0, 3, 6, 9, 12, 15, or 18 seconds. In order to prevent participants from rehearsing the consonants during the interval (which would have extended the duration of the STM) they were asked to count backwards aloud in threes from a three-digit number they were given. It is worthwhile trying this. The sequence is as follows:

Exercise

First, get a friend to present you with a trigram (e.g. N H W), immediately followed by a three-digit number such as 456. Count backwards from that number in threes aloud (456, 453, 450, etc.) until your friend gives you the signal (a tap on the table will do) for you to recall the trigram. Then repeat the three letters. You can repeat this with various time lapses.

The Trace Decay Theory of Forgetting

The Petersons found that correct recall was high after short intervals such as 3 or 6 seconds, but by 18 seconds interval participants were recalling only about 10 per cent correctly. They suggested that the duration of STM was only about 6 to 12 seconds if unrehearsed. There was a memory trace within the brain which decayed gradually. This was the trace decay theory of forgetting.

Interference Theory of Forgetting

An alternative explanation for this phenomenon was that forgetting occurred when other material interfered with memorisation. The Patersons found that while the first set of consonants in a series of trials was not often forgotten, in later trials participants began to mix up the trigrams they were asked to recall. This was an interference theory of forgetting.

Coding in STM

It is clear that immediate memory is either iconic or echoic, depending on whether the information was received visually or aurally. Evidence has been produced by Conrad (1964) that STM is coded acoustically: that is to say, what matters is what the material to be recalled sounds like. In his experiments, 387 participants were shown sequences of six letters on a screen and were told to write them down as they appeared. However they were presented too fast for them to keep up, so that they had partly to be held in memory. In some cases, participants substituted wrong letters. Conrad did an analysis of these errors and concluded that in most cases participants substituted letters which sounded similar (B for V or X for S, for example). These acoustic confusion errors suggested that STM was coded acoustically, even when the original material had been presented visually. There must be a means of re-coding material, presented visually, for it to be registered in the sound-based STM.

Visual Coding in STM

Den Heyer and Barrett (1971) have, however, produced evidence for visual or visuo-spatial coding in STM. Participants in their experiment were presented with a grid pattern with letters on it at random. They had to recall two things:

- The letters on the grid.
- The position in the grid where letters occurred.

As with the Petersons' experiments, there were tasks interposed between the presentation of the array and the recall (either a 'counting backwards' task or else a visual 'matching patterns' task). While the 'counting backwards' task disrupted recall of the letters on the grid, recall of the positions of letters on the grid was interfered with most by the 'visual matching' task. The conclusion they reached was that the letters were coded verbally, whereas the positions were coded visually.

Long-term Memory

This is the final stage in the modal model. While it is possible to characterise short-term memory in terms of its duration, its capacity and its coding it is much more difficult to do this for long-term memory. There seem to be no known limits to the duration or to the capacity of long-term memory storage. It is important that semantic connections (that is to say, understanding of meaning) are involved in the process of coding for long-term memory, but that is not the only way in which it is organised. There is great diversity, not only in what is stored – all kinds of knowledge and beliefs, objects and events, people and places, plans and skills – but also how it is stored. This section will examine some of the factors involved in organisation and retrieval in long-term memory, including distinctions between **episodic** and **semantic** memory, **interference effects** and the ways in which it seems that material is organised within our memory systems. It is worthwhile to remind readers of the stages involved in memory, because recall or forgetting may be influenced at each or any stage. These are the **input or encoding stage**, the **storage stage** and the **retrieval stage**.

Episodic and Semantic Memory

The model of memory proposed by Tulving (1972) suggests a distinction between episodic and semantic memory. The distinction seems to be as follows.

Episodic Memory

The storage of information about events and the relationships between them has been described as episodic memory. Here are some examples:

1. There was a gale last winter and tiles crashed down from the roof on to the patio.
2. At Easter, we visited our grandchildren who were staying in Yorkshire.
3. Unfortunately I had left the lights of the car on and when I returned the battery was flat.

Each of these examples are episodes which describe personal experiences. Memory for them is related to other experiences. Leaving the car lights on is related, for instance, to coming back to find the battery flat and the car refusing to start.

Semantic Memory

While episodic memory is memory for fairly transitory events in your experience, semantic memory can be described as memory for more permanent items of knowledge, usually involving language, such as: (a) it is usually warmer in the summer than in the winter; (b) a starling and a robin are birds, but a bat is a mammal which flies; or (c) $2 + 2 = 4$.

Tulving has defined semantic memory as:

A mental thesaurus, organised knowledge a person possesses about words and other verbal symbols, their meanings and referents, about relations among them, and about rules, formulas and algorithms for the manipulation of these symbols, concepts and relations. Semantic memory does not register perceptible properties of inputs, but rather cognitive referents of input signals (Tulving, 1972, p. 386).

The distinctions which Tulving made between these forms of memory involve a wide range of characteristics. Tulving (1983) lists 28 different distinctions. Episodic memory, for example, is based upon sensations, semantic memory upon understanding; episodic memory is time related, semantic memory is related to concepts; episodic memory is very subject to forgetting, semantic memory is less so; semantic memory tends to be more useful to an individual than episodic memory.

Some Criticisms

Johnson and Hasher (1987) contend that episodic and semantic memory have not been shown empirically to be separate systems which can be isolated from one another. Wood *et al.* (1980) in support of Tulving has shown that there were different bloodflow patterns in the left cerebral hemisphere for participants in their experiment who were engaged on a episodic memory task from that for other participants who were engaged on a semantic memory task. However, it was pointed out by critics (Baddeley, 1984; McKoon *et al.*, 1986) that any two different tasks, even two semantic tasks, might be accompanied by different bloodflow patterns. It did not imply that there was a distinction between semantic and episodic memory.

Some of Tulving's distinctive characteristics were also called into question by McKoon and her colleagues. Tulving had claimed, for instance, that semantic memory was conceptual; episodic memory was time related. Ratcliff and McKoon (1978) showed that even in episodic memory conceptual relationships may be as important as time relationships.

Interference Effects

One of the factors which seems to influence whether something is forgotten or not is interference. Where there is some similarity between one lot of material remembered and another, recall can be affected. Interference effects can be of one of two kinds.

1. **Retroactive interference** occurs when what you learn later interferes with previously stored material. You have perhaps learned the times of the trains to London and then you look up in a train timetable when trains leave for Birmingham. This new learning may interfere with the old and cause you to forget it.
2. **Proactive interference** works the other way around. The stored memory you have for the times of trains to London may interfere with and cause you to forget train times to Birmingham.

McGeoch and Macdonald (1931) demonstrated retroactive interference effects in an early experiment. Participants were divided into five experimental and one control group. All groups were given a list of words to learn. The five experimental groups were then given another learning task. They had to learn either: (a) numbers; (b) nonsense syllables; (c) words unrelated to the original list; (d) synonyms of the words in the original list; (e) antonyms of the words in the original list.

The control group had no intervening task. When recall of the original list was tested, success varied from 4.5 for the control group to 1.25 for those who had to learn synonyms. There seemed to have been more interference where the material was similar. More words were remembered by the group which had to learn numbers (3.68) than nonsense syllables (2.58), unrelated words (2.17) or antonyms (1.83).

Organisation in Long-term Memory

There will inevitably be a very complex mass of information stored in LTM. Without some organisation much of this material will become inaccessible to recall. It seems likely that items in the long term memory are grouped together according to their meanings, Free-recall studies allow participants to recall material in any order they wish. It is then possible for experimenters to see how material is grouped in the memory.

Bousfield (1953) gave participants 60 items to learn in a random order. The list included 15 names of animals, 15 names of people, 15 professions and 15 vegetables. They were asked to recall the list in any order they liked. Participants tended to remember them in clusters, belonging to the same category. Once they had remembered one animal, for instance, several others tended to follow. Bousfield suggested that there must be some kind of semantic organisation in long-term memory.

As well as **semantic categorisation** there seems also to be some organisation into **hierarchies**. Bower *et al.* (1969) divided participants into two groups and asked them to learn a list of 112 words. Under one condition, the words were already organised into four different conceptual hierarchies as illustrated in Figure 4.2 below.

In the other condition participants received the same words, arranged in a similar pattern, but the words were not organised into

---

FIGURE 4.2

A Hierarchy of Animals

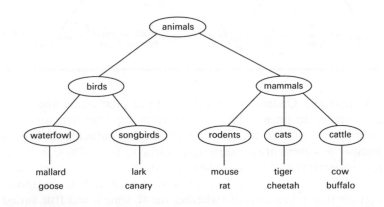

hierarchies. In the first learning trial the first group remembered 65 per cent of the words as opposed to 18 per cent for the other group. After three trials recall was 100 per cent for the first group as compared with 47 per cent for the other group. Organisation into a hierarchical form seems to have a dramatic effect upon recall.

A extension of this has been Collins and Quillian's (1969) **network model of semantic memory**. A network consists of a series of nodes with links between them. A name is linked to some characteristic. For instance, 'bird' is linked to 'has wings' or 'can fly'. The network is hierarchical in the same way that Bower *et al.*'s conceptual hierarchies are. An example of Collins and Quillian's hierarchical organisation model is illustrated in Figure 4.3.

FIGURE 4.3

Collins and Quillian's Hierarchical Model of Memory Organisation

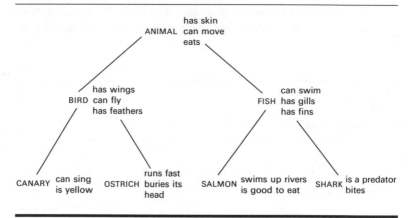

Collins and Quillian were able to make predictions about the time needed to retrieve information from the long-term store. A technique employed consisted of presenting participants with a number of statements to be judged as true or false. These included true statements like the ones above and also some false ones like 'canaries have gills'. Response times were measured. It was found that the time taken to verify whether the statement was true varied with the number of levels of the hierarchy the search has to pass through. You could predict, for instance, that 'a canary can sing' would take less time to verify than 'a salmon has gills'. In the first case, there is just one level involved, in the second case two. A statement such as 'a shark has skin' would take longer still to verify as there are three levels involved. It seems that in the last case the memory search has to pass through three stages 'a shark is a fish', 'a fish is an animal', and 'an animal has skin'.

Exercise

Using Collins and Quillian's network (Figure 4.3) which of the following statements would take longest to verify:
    an ostrich eats;
    a salmon spawns in rivers;
    birds can breathe?

Typicality Effect

There is a problem with Collins and Quillian's model in that it seems to work very well with a typical member of a category (a cod is a fish, for example) but less well for untypical members of a category (a penguin is a bird, for example). It has been found that a statement about a typical member of a group may be verified faster than one about an untypical member.

Spreading Activation Model

Problems such as the above have led Collins and Loftus (1975) to suggest a different kind of network model. They termed this a **spreading activation** model. In this model concepts are grouped in interconnected clusters rather than hierarchically. Closely related concepts share many links and lie close together so that the paths between them are short. 'Bird' and 'wings' and 'sparrow' would probably lie close together in memory storage and would have many interconnecting links. 'Shark' and 'yellow' and 'feathers' would not lie so closely together and would not have so many links. The important points about this model seem to be the following:

1. Speed of access depends on the length and strength of the links.
2. Strength of linkage depends on frequency of use.
3. Activation of memory about concepts spreads outwards to adjacent concepts (from 'birds to 'wings' to 'feathers', for instance).
4. As the distance increases so the strength of the activation decreases. There is no indefinite spread of activation. No matter how long you took over it, it is unlikely that thinking about roses would lead you to think about lions! The paths between are too long and too indirect.

This model has distinct advantages over the earlier network models. Typicality is not a problem. It also links in very well with what is already known about how information is represented in the brain. Activation of a concept can be thought of as activating a neuron (or nerve cell). The activation then spreads to other neurons producing a pattern of excitation. While such patterns do not last long, there is also evidence for longer-term changes in the ways in which nerve cells are linked to each other, their synaptic connections. These may make particular links easier or harder to excite.

A Commentary on the Modal Model of Memory

There are several points which need to be made about this model of memory:

1. The model implies that there is a one-way flow of information, from immediate memory to short-term and finally to long-term stores. But this is not necessarily the case. Suppose that you were registering the letter V in the short-term memory (from a spelling of a name in a phone conversation perhaps). You would need to equate the letter V with the sound 'vee'. That relationship you would have stored in your long-term memory. There must therefore be a link back from LTM to STM.
2. The model emphasises the amount of information which is stored. Common sense would suggest that it is at least as important to consider what kind of material has to be remembered. Some things are easier to remember than others. Information which is funny, familiar, distinctive or which has

some particular association for us (a self reference perhaps) is more easily recalled. Meaningful material is remembered much more readily than that which has no meaning for us.

3. The model ignores the fairly crucial point that there are enormous individual differences in the way we operate our memories.

4. Another vital point is that the model pays no attention to the function of memory. While emphasising what memory does and how it works it ignores what it is for. A later section in this chapter will look at the operation of memory in everyday life, the ecology of memory.

5. There is not universal acceptance of a distinction between short-term and long-term memory storage. Depth of processing theories, for example, which will be discussed later, blur this distinction. However, clinical evidence from patients suffering from Korsakov's syndrome (where chronic alcoholism produces a combination of dementia and amnesia) or from those who have sustained a severe head injury, shows that STM can sometimes be severely impaired while LTM remains intact.

6. The model understates the complexity of LTM.

Some Alternatives to the Modal Model

Working Memory Model (Baddeley and Hitch, 1974)

The model of memory which we have been considering up to now envisages passive storage of information. Immediate, short-term and long-term stores have storage durations which vary, as well as varying capacities. The **working memory model** takes a more active view of memory. It is concerned with the storage of information which is being used actively and about which we are currently thinking. This may come from two sources: (a) new sensory information; (b) old information stored in the long-term memory. For instance, if you were replacing the sparking plugs in your car you use new sensory information to locate the spanner over the plug and old stored information as to which way to turn the spanner to unscrew it.

Baddeley (1981) has suggested that working memory consists of several parts as illustrated in Figure 4.4.

FIGURE 4.4

The Working Memory Model

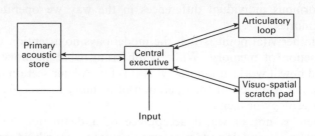

1. An articulatory loop which stores material in verbal form and allows for verbal rehearsal (the inner voice).
2. A primary acoustic store of limited capacity which accepts material either directly as it is heard or via the articulatory loop (the inner ear)
3. A visuo-spatial scratchpad which allows for intake of visual information and for visual and spatial rehearsal.
4. A central executive, free of sense modality.

To relate the working memory model to what has been discussed under the heading of short-term memory, consider the articulatory loop as explaining how seven (plus or minus two) items of information can be stored for a brief period (6–12 seconds), unless rehearsal takes place. The loop allows for this rehearsal. Baddeley experimented with articulatory suppression. Participants were made to mutter some words or phrases to occupy and suppress the articulatory loop, while at the same time performing another task such as learning a list of words. Where it was found that this procedure of **concurrent verbalisation** impaired performance of the task, it was assumed that the articulatory loop was employed in the task. This is not unlike the Petersons' technique for preventing rehearsal. The visuo-spatial scratch pad is the visual equivalent of the articulatory loop and explains Den Heyer and Barrett's findings, mentioned above (p. 101).

An Evaluation of the Working Memory Model

There are positive and negative points to be made:

1. On the positive side, it can be said to come much closer to explaining how memory actually works than the Atkinson/ Shiffrin model does. For instance, by the suggestion that there are different ways of dealing with different kinds of information (sound-based, verbal, visual or spatial). It is also useful to see a common source of resources in the central executive used in widely different cognitive tasks. It begins to be possible to see how memory systems may operate in such diverse tasks as reading and doing mental arithmetic. In reading, the articulatory loop has been seen to be involved alongside the central executive which oversees semantic analysis and the comprehension of the material (Baddeley and Lewis, 1981). It is an active rather than a passive system and has more ecological validity as it can be seen to involve real-life tasks.

2. There are two unresolved problems:
    (a) It is not very clear exactly what role the central executive plays. It is claimed to have a limited capacity yet there has been no measurement of that capacity. It is said to be modality free, but how it operates has not been defined.
    (b) The clear distinctions which have been made between the various components seem rather unrealistic. Baddeley and Lewis (1981) in their investigation of the operation of working memory in reading found that the speed and accuracy of judgements about the sounds of words and non-words was unaffected by articulatory suppression. This kind of processing of sounds was taking place somewhere other than in the articulatory loop.

Levels of Processing

A second alternative is the **levels of processing** model proposed by Craik and Lockhart (1972). Their thesis is that information memorised is processed at different levels which relate to what is done with the material. Processing is either **shallow** or **deep** and this processing level determines how well the material is retained.

Shallow Processing

Shallow processing consists simply of coding the material (structurally) in terms of its physical characteristics, such things, for example, as whether a word is written in upper or lower-case type or acoustically (according to its sound). This could be, for instance, whether the voice is that of a man or a woman.

Deep Processing

Where the processing involves some semantic manipulation (that is, manipulation which relates to its meaning) then there is a deeper level of processing. For instance, answering the question of whether 'bear' means the same as 'carry' would involve some semantic processing. It focuses on the meaning of the words.

It is assumed that the retention of material is dependent directly upon the depth at which it has been processed. It is not realistic to make a sharp distinction between Short Term and Long Term Memory. Stimuli undergo successive processing operations, at first in terms of physical characteristics (the letters and the typeface of a printed word or the sound of a spoken word), then at a deeper level in terms of meaning. It is perhaps interesting to compare this with some of the ideas developed about attention, discussed in Chapter 2, which separate processing of physical characteristics from deeper semantic processing. Rehearsal of material to be remembered can also be at different depths:

- simple repetition is shallow and is termed **maintenance rehearsal**; and
- when rehearsal explores meaning, it is termed **elaborative rehearsal** and involves deep processing.

While shallow processing leads to short term retention, deep processing leads to longer term retention.

Elias and Perfetti (1973) gave participants in an experiment a list of words. For some of the words they were asked to find rhymes, for others they had to produce synonyms. While they were not specifically asked to memorise the words, they were subsequently tested on how many they could recall. It was found that they could recall significantly more of those words for which they had had to produce synonyms. This, of course, involved semantic processing, while finding rhymes involved just the sound of the words and so was shallow processing. Craik and Tulving (1975) found that people who had answered questions about a word's meaning were about three times as likely to recall it later as they would be if they had simply answered questions about the word's physical characteristics. Other forms of memory, too, seem to be affected by this deep/shallow processing distinction. Groups of participants in an experiment conducted by Fiske and Schneider (1984) were each given different instructions for dealing with stimuli with which they were presented:

- Some had to press a button whenever they detected a word which represented the name of a vehicle (semantic processing).
- Others had to press the button whenever the word contained the letter G (graphic processing).
- Others again were told to ignore the words altogether (control).

After participants had seen all the stimuli, Fiske and Schneider asked them to estimate how many times they had seen each of the words. There was a clear relationship between estimates and processing instructions. In the vehicle-naming condition (semantic processing), a word presented 20 times was reported as having been presented 18 times, while in the letter G condition (graphic processing) only 5 times and in the 'ignore' condition 0 times.

Originally Craik and Lockhart had only concerned themselves with the encoding end of memory and not with retrieval. A later piece of research, however, suggested that the same distinction should also apply to retrieval (Moscovitch and Craik, 1976). The reasons why deep processing seems to influence recall relate, in the view of Craik and Lockhart (1986), to two factors:

1. **Distinctiveness**, which describes the extent to which a stimulus is different from other memory traces in the system.
2. **Elaboration**, that is, how rich the processing is in terms of meaning.

Let us take some examples:

Suppose you want to remember the word 'chicken'. If processing involved the notion of a chicken strolling down the motorway dodging the cars as they raced by, that would provide a more distinctive memory trace than, say, a chicken sitting on a nest and laying an egg.

If this image was elaborated upon by suggesting that the chicken on the motorway had a bare behind because it had lost all its tail feathers and was being chased by an irate farmer brandishing a pitchfork it would be very memorable!

Research by Craik and Tulving (1975) emphasises the importance of elaboration. Participants were asked to read sentences and decide which words were appropriate in the sentences. Some were simple, such as:

She cooked the - - - -

Others were more elaborate like:

The great bird swooped down and carried off the struggling - - - -

The accompanying words were either appropriate (rabbit) or inappropriate (book). Recall was much better where the sentence frame was more elaborate.

All this research seems very much divorced from the reality of anything you might ever have to remember. Palmere *et al.* (1983) have shown that it need not be so. Participants were made to read a 32-paragraph essay on a fictitious African nation. Each paragraph contained just one major idea and consisted of four sentences, one 'main idea' sentence and three others which provided examples of the main idea. As they were presented to participants, eight of the paragraphs were intact, eight had one example sentence removed, eight had two example sentences removed, eight had all three example sentences removed. Participants read the essay and were tested on their recall of the main ideas. The greater the elaboration, the more examples, the greater was the recall of the main ideas.

Self-referencing Effect

Recall of material seems to be better when there is **self reference**, that is to say when individuals can relate it to themselves. This has been regarded as an extension of the levels of processing approach to the study of memory. Rogers *et al.* (1977) asked participants in their study to process lists of words with much the same kinds of instructions as in other research into levels of processing. There were instructions which related to the physical characteristics of the words (capital or small letters, for instance), instructions which related to acoustic properties of the words (rhyming perhaps), instructions which demanded that participants consider the meanings of the words and also self-referencing instructions. These required participants to decide whether a particular word could be applied to themselves. It was found that the greatest number of words recalled were those which had self-referencing instructions. For the rest, the results were predictable, the next best recall being for words with semantic instructions, then acoustic and finally physical instructions.

There are clearly possible practical applications for this. Apart from the obvious one that a good way of remembering material presented to you is to relate it to yourself, there is a suggestion in a study by D'Ydewalle *et al.* (1985) which suggests that products might be better remembered by inviting consumers to consider how they might use the product themselves.

An Evaluation of the Depth of Processing Approach

1. It has been suggested that this approach represents an over-simplification of what is in fact a very complex reality. We have seen that there are several different ways in which 'depth' can be interpreted. The **amount of effort** which is put into it, for instance. Tyler *et al.* (1979) had participants in their experiment solving two sets of anagrams, easy ones or more difficult ones. While the level of processing in each case seemed to be the same, they remembered more of the difficult anagrams than of the easy ones. We have already seen that others have highlighted factors such as elaboration or distinctiveness.

2. Eysenck suggests that the arguments might be circular ones.

> In view of the vagueness with which depth is defined, there is danger of using retention-test performance to provide information about depth of processing, and then using the putative 'depth of processing' to explain retention test performance (Eysenck, 1978, p. 159).

3. Craik and Lockhart have tended to use only free-recall as a retention test. Morris *et al.* (1977) have used either a standard recognition test or else a rhyming recognition test, where partici-

pants had to select words which rhymed with the words in the list. While the standard test produced results which were in line with what the depth of processing hypothesis would predict, the rhyming recognition test showed that more words were recognised where the instructions involved processing the words acoustically. This could be, for instance, asking 'does the word rhyme with - - - -?' rather than when the instructions involved semantic processing (e.g. asking 'does the word mean the same as?'). Shallow processing seemed to be producing better memory for the words than deep processing.

Morris *et al.* (1977) suggested that different kinds of processing led learners to acquire different kinds of information. Retention depends on whether the information acquired is relevant to the kind of test used.

4. It has been assumed that deeper levels of processing are associated with more durable memory for information. It is not possible to test whether this is true without ensuring that the amount of learning at different depths of processing is the same. This has not usually been done. However, when Nelson and Vining (1978) manipulated the number of learning trials so that there was equal learning at deep and shallow levels of processing there was the same rate of forgetting with deep as with shallow processing.

Self-assessment Questions

1. What are the three stages in Atkinson and Shiffrin's model of memory? How do they differ:
   (i) in terms of coding?
   (ii) in terms of duration?
2. Does Craik and Lockhart's 'depth of processing' theory seem to you to replace the need to assume separate short-term and long-term memory stores?
3. Describe Baddeley's 'working memory model'. Do you feel it gets over the problems thrown up by the 'modal' model?
4. How did Tulving distinguish between semantic and episodic memory. List two distinctions.
5. Distiguish between retroactive and proactive interference.
6. Compare the models of memory organisation of Bower *et al.*, Collins and Quillian and Collins and Loftus. How do the main features of each differ?

SECTION III REAL-LIFE MEMORY

In this section we shall examine memory for events in one's own past (autobiographical memory), remembering to do things and eye-witness testimony. All these things are more closely related to reality than the laboratory studies discussed up to now.

Autobiographical Memory

We have considered the way in which semantic memory seems to be organised. **Autobiographical** memory is concerned with episodic memory. It is the memory for events in a person's life. Research into autobiographical memory tends not to deal with lists of words or nonsense syllables. It also tends to be conducted not in laboratories but 'in the field'. There is emphasis on **ecological validity**.

Parallel to Ebbinghaus's studies of his own memory in the last century (Section I of this chapter) Linton (1982, 1986) tested her own memory for events which had occurred in her own life. Each day she recorded two events which had occurred during the day and each month tested her memory for those events. She looked at each brief description of events and attempted to recognise exactly the event described, together with its date. In six years she accumulated 5500 events. She found that her memory for real life events faded only about 5 per cent a year. Pleasant memories were easiest to recall with about 50 per cent correctly recalled; about 30 per cent of unpleasant events and 20 per cent of neutral ones were correctly remembered.

Accuracy of Recall

The accuracy with which we recall events in our lives depends on several things:

1. the time which has elapsed since the event.;
2. the type of event, whether pleasant, unpleasant or neutral; and
3. whether the event occurred to oneself or to another person.

Other factors which have been researched include **search strategy, the position of an event in a longer sequence** and the **cues used to**

trigger recall (Loftus and Fathi, 1986). Seaching one's memory, starting with most recent events and working backwards seems to be more accurate than the other way around. Pillemer *et al.* (1986) found that students recalled events which occurred early in the college year more accurately than those later in the year. Rubin *et al.* (1984) found that odours evoked unique memories more than other cues.

Lapse of Time

Thompson (1982) found that accuracy in dating events decreased by more than a day for each week that passed. For instance, after two weeks had passed people were inaccurate by about two days, but after 10 weeks this inaccuracy had increased to 12 days.

Pleasant or Unpleasant Events

Thompson (1985) also noted that pleasant events were recalled more accurately than unpleasant ones (but then, they were also rated as being more memorable).

Self-reference Effect

There seems to be a **self reference effect** in memory for life events as well as for words. Thompson *et al.* (1987) found that where events actually happened to them, individuals remembered dates more accurately than if they occurred to someone else.

Flashbulb Memory

The term **flashbulb memory** has been used to refer to our memory for the situation in which we first learned of an outstanding event. For instance, people are said to have very accurate memories of what they were doing when they heard that President Kennedy had been shot.

Brown and Kulik (1977) attempted to investigate this by questioning people to see whether certain national events triggered this kind of memory. They listed six kinds of information which were likely to be listed in flashbulb memories for national events:

(a)   the place;
(b)   the event that was interrupted by the news;
(c)   the person who gave them the news;
(d)   their feelings;
(e)   the feelings of others;
(f)   the aftermath.

Brown and Kulik found that what determined the triggering of flashbulb memories included first and foremost a high level of surprise, a perception of the importance of the event and the high level of emotional arousal which accompanied it.

More recently Pillemer (1984) asked people to recall the attempted assassination of President Reagan on 30 March 1981. First, a month after the event and then again six months later participants were asked where they were at the time of the assassination attempt and who told them about it. There was quite vivid recall of individuals' personal situation at the time of the attempt. There were strong visual images. The amount of the emotion which the event aroused in individuals seemed to be positively related to the vividness, elaboration and consistency with which the detail was recalled.

Rubin and Kozin (1984) also studied vivid memories for events in people's lives. Participants were asked to describe the three clearest memories from their past. The categories of memories they reported were interesting: 18 per cent concerned accidents or injuries to themselves or their friends. Other frequently reported memories included sports, love affairs, animals and things which happened to them in their first weeks at college. National events only figured in 3 per cent of memories. The most vivid memories were the most surprising and the ones which were most rehearsed.

Schematisation of Autobiographical Memory

Schemata represent generalisations abstracted from a large number of specific events in our lives and serve to summarise important attributes in the events. Suppose you developed a schema for lunchtimes. Attributes might include where you consistently tend to sit to eat lunch, who you tend to eat with and the topics of conversation which arise. This schematisation provides organisation so that we can summarise events in our lives. Single events are not readily distinguishable. If you are asked to recall details they are likely to be reconstructions of the generic or schematic memory. You may recall events which never happened, but which are similar to the schemata you have developed. Neisser (1981) has termed this inaccurate memorisation of events **repisodic memory**. This is an example of cognitve processes actively reshaping our memories. Barclay (1986) has provided some empirical evidence for this. Three graduate students were asked to keep records of three memorable events a day. At a later date they were presented with accounts of events which were either exactly what they had written or a 'foil', a similar but unfamiliar event. Approximately half of these foils were recognised as having occurred.

Remembering to Do Things

While there has been much research into **retrospective memory**, that is memory for things previously learned, **prospective memory** or memory for future actions already planned (remembering to do things) has been much less well-researched. One area which has received some attention is **absent-mindedness**. Reason (1984) notes that these kinds of slips of memory are more likely to occur:

1. in familiar surroundings;
2. if you are pre-occupied;
3. if there are other distractions;
4. if there is pressure of time; and
5. if a well-established routine is changed. For instance, if you have decided to have croissants for breakfast instead of toast and they are all ready for you, you may still automatically make your customary pieces of toast!

Meacham and Singer (1977) gave students eight postcards to send back to the experimenter one a week for eight weeks. There were two conditions:

1. Some participants had instructions that they should send them back every Wednesday.
2. Others had to send them back on a specified different day each week.

In each of these two groups some were told they would receive payment ($5) for remembering to send back the cards, while others received no payment. While the 'every Wednesday' group were no better at remembering to return them than the 'random day' group, a promised payment did make a difference. A further study (Harris, 1984) indicated that the interval between being given instructions and carrying them out made little difference. People instructed to return cards two days later were no more reliable than those who had a 36-day delay.

Eyewitness Testimony

The unreliability of testimony in court from those who have been eyewitnesses to an event is well-attested. However, juries still seem willing to trust the testimony of eyewitnesses. Perhaps they should be more careful. There are two problems:

1. Being able to recognise faces accurately.
2. Associated with this, the difficulty of recall of other information relating to an event.

Section I of this chapter included discussion of Bartlett's study of reconstructive memory. Some of the issues involved are similar to those relating to eye-witness testimony. Detail tends to be rationalised to fit the way in which the individual has conceived the event.

Recognition of Faces

In Chapter 3 there was a discussion of pattern recognition and in particular, feature analysing models of pattern recognition (pp. 51–2). This is relevant here. There have also been studies which have dealt particularly with the problems of recognising faces. Shapiro and Penrod (1986) collated the results of 128 studies of facial recognition in order to see whether any particular variable seems to have an effect on accuracy of recognition. The following factors seem to have a bearing on this:

1. People seem to recognise members of their own race significantly better than members of another race.

2. The more time and attention which is spent upon looking at a face, the greater the accuracy of recognition.
3. Accuracy of recognition is likely to be reduced where something distracts attention from the face.
4. The upper part of a person's face determines recognition of it to a markedly greater extent than the lower half of the face.
5. Some of the factors discussed in the section on depth of processing (pp. 111–16) also seem to apply here. Where it has been necessary to make some judgement about a face, recognition is likely to be more accurate than when a person simply looks at a face.
6. Training does not seem to influence accuracy of recognition.
7. The length of time which has elapsed does not seem to influence accuracy of recognition automatically. Depth of processing and the distinctiveness of the face seem more important in increasing accuracy. What has happened in the interval also matters. Presenting other pictures of faces, or photo-fits, substantially reduces accuracy.

Recall of Circumstances

Witnesses to motor accidents are frequently asked to recall the details of what happened. Loftus and Palmer (1974) showed that the wording of a question relating to what a witness had seen could make a substantial difference to the accuracy of testimony. Participants in their study were shown a film of a multiple car accident. After being asked to describe what happened in their own words they were asked specific questions. There were three groups:

1. some were asked, 'About how fast were the cars going when they smashed into each other?'
2. others were asked, 'About how fast were the cars going when they hit each other?'
3. a control group were not asked any question about the speed of the cars.

The first group's mean estimate of the cars' speed was 10.5 mph, the second group's estimate was 8.0 mph The wording of the question had affected the recall of the motor accident. A week later all the participants were asked the question: 'Did you see any broken glass?' Even though there was no broken glass shown in the film of the accident, 32 per cent of the first group said that there was broken glass, compared to 14 per cent of the second group and 12 per cent of the control group. Eyewitness evidence is easily distorted by information presented subsequently. The explanation that participants may simply have been responding to the experimental situation, arguing that cars that smash into each other would inevitably produce broken glass, has been refuted by a later experiment.

Several groups of participants in an experiment by Loftus *et al.* (1978) saw slides of a sports car which stopped at an intersection and then turned and hit a pedestrian. Of these groups:

Group A saw a 'stop' sign at the intersection.
Group B saw a 'yield' sign.

Twenty minutes to one week later participants were asked questions about the accident. A critical question contained information which was either:

1. consistent;
2. inconsistent with the detail of what they had seen on the slides;
3. alternatively, the detail was not mentioned in the question.

For instance, members of the group which had seen the 'stop' sign were asked 'Did another car pass the red Datsun while it was stopped at the "yield" sign?' (inconsistent). Other members of the group were asked, 'Did another car pass the red Datsun while it was stopped at the "stop" sign?' (consistent). Still other members of the group had a question which did not include the sign at all. Then they were shown slides, one with a 'stop' sign and one with a 'yield' sign and asked which they had seen. Those who had had an inconsistent question tended to choose the information contained in the questionnaire rather than that on the original slides. Those who had had a consistent or a neutral question produced more correct responses. Later information does influence the responses of eyewitnesses.

Attempts have been made, in the two studies below, to find out how people can be made to resist information which may distort their memory:

1. Greene *et al.* (1982) showed that warnings about the possibility of misinformation, when responding to a questionnaire, may increase accuracy. The time taken to read the questionnaire also seems to have a bearing on this.
2. Tousignant *et al.* (1986) found that those who took their time to read the questionnaire were more likely to be accurate than those who did it hastily.

This section has contained some of the more ecologically-valid pieces of research which have emerged as a result of Neisser's strictures about memory research (Neisser 1982) in a speech in which he refers to the 'thundering silence' for the previous hundred years on real memory.

> You need only tell a friend, not himself a psychologist, that you study memory. Given a little encouragement, your friend will describe all sorts of interesting phenomena: the limitations of his memory for early childhood, his inability to remember appoint-ments, his aunt who could recite poems from memory by the hour, the regrettable decline in his ability to remember names, how well he could find his way around his home town after a thirty years' absence, the differences between his memory and someone else's. Our research has, of course, virtually nothing to say about any of these topics (Neisser, 1982).

The concluding section of this chapter will contain some practical ideas for the improvement of memory skills.

Self-assessment Questions

1. List some of the factors found by Linton to influence the accuracy of memory for events in our lives.
2. What are some of the factors which seem to have a bearing on ability to recognise faces accurately?
3. In what ways can later information distort memory for events of which a person has been an eyewitness?

SECTION VI   HOW TO IMPROVE YOUR MEMORY

This section is devoted to techniques which may improve recall of information. For the most part it is firmly based upon research and what is known about the way in which memory works. There are two broad categories in which these techniques lie, first the use of **imagery** and second the employment of **organisational strategies**.

Using Imagery to Assist your Memory

Imagery involves creating in the mind mental pictures of things which are not physically present. Clearly, it is much easier to represent some things with mental pictures than others. Concrete objects, such as a 'house', a 'chair' or an 'envelope' (**high imagery material**) are much easier to picture than abstracts such as 'justice' or the 'balance of payments deficit' (**low imagery material**). Paivio (1968) showed that people will ordinarily recall high imagery material twice as well as low imagery material. Bower (1972) asked participants in his experiment to memorise pairs of unrelated words. One group (the experimental group) was asked to make mental images of the pairs of words (for instance, if the two words were 'shoe' and 'orange' the mental image created might show a shoe with an orange prominently attached to the toe). The control group was merely asked to memorise the words. The experimental group showed significantly better recall of the pairs of words. Bower also noted that the more unusual the images were, the better was the recall. We noted in the section concerned with levels of processing (pp. 111–16) that deeper processing with more elaboration and with self-referencing is likely to result in more accurate recall. The more active the manipulation of representations of what you are trying to remember, the more effective the recall. It is also important to note that long-term memory is very dependent upon organisation. Things are better remembered linked together than unrelated. It might be well to refer back to the section on long term memory organisation on pp. 104–8.

One way, therefore to improve memorisation, is to create mental images of things which have to be remembered and then associate these with other mental images. These can either be things which you wish to remember as associated ('justice' perhaps, represented by the scales on the Old Bailey building), or, alternatively, it is possible to create a list of items which are memorable to you in some way and then pair each item in that list with something which you want to remember, making a careful mental picure in your mind of each pair together. A list of ten items which has been much used and is well known to most people rhymes the numbers one to ten:

one	bun
two	shoe
three	tree
four	door
five	hive
six	sticks
seven	heaven
eight	gate
nine	line
ten	hen

It is easy enough to remember the rhyming words and then to create images which associate each with an item you wish to remember. This can be extended almost indefinitely, by, for instance, creating an alphabetical list of, say, animals:

A is for antelope
B is for bear
C is for cat
D is for dog

and so on

The alphabetical list will be comparatively easy to learn and then images of each animal can be placed in your mind alongside images of the things you have to remember. There can, of course be many alphabetical lists. It has been suggested that this kind of imagery will be assisted if the images created are as bizarre as possible. The research evidence on this is not clear-cut. Wollen *et al.* (1972) found that it mattered more for recall that the images created interacted with each other than that they were bizarre. Other studies such as that of Weber and Marshall (1978) found that bizarreness did make a difference especially when there was some delay in recall.

The applications of this kind of imagery are wide ranging. It has been used by Patten (1972) with patients with memory disorders. It has been used extensively in the teaching of foreign languages. Atkinson and Raugh (1975) asked students to think of English words which resembled each of the Russian words they were trying to teach and then create images of the English word interacting with the meaning of the Russian word. Bull and Wittrock (1973) found that imagery helped children extend their vocabulary. Children had to draw pictures of the new words and then write definitions of them.

Method of Loci

Cicero, a Roman orator of the first century BC was known to have used the **method of loci** to remember names and other facts he needed to remember in his speeches. He visualised the people and facts which he needed to remember; in particular, locations around the room in which he was speaking. More recently, Bower (1970) has outlined how this technique might be used. The first stage is to identify and commit to memory a number of specific locations. You might use the route followed as you go from home to college. Along this route will be landmarks that can be used for locations (the point where you have to turn off the main road on to a foot path, for instance). At each of these locations, mentally re-created in imagery in your mind, place an image of something which you need to remember. Then all that is needed is to traverse the route in your mind and the objects which you have placed along it will come to mind.

Groninger (1971) tested this technique experimentally. Participants in this study operated under two conditions. In the experimental condition, they had to think of 25 locations in order. Then items on a 25-word list were mentally pictured at each of these locations. Participants in the control condition were free to use any method they wished to memorise the 25-word list in order. There was to be no further rehearsal of the word list. Then, after intervals of one week and five weeks both groups were tested. Recall of the word lists was significantly better for those who used the method of loci than for the control group, particularly after five weeks.

Extensions of this method have been tried by Bellezza (1983). Words on a page, set out, each with a distinctive arrangement on the page were learned more easily than if they did not have this distinctive arrangement or pattern on the page. In a later study, Bellezza (1986) found participants learnt abstract psychology terms more easily if they were superimposed on a picture. For example a cue word, depth for instance, in 'depth perception', could be illustrated by a drawing of a steep cliff with someone at the top and the bottom of it. Associated words like relative size, light and shade and texture could be arranged around it.

Lovelace and Southall (1983) found that students remembered material better when it was presented to them typed on pages with numbers and space at the top and bottom of the page. Knowledge of where the material was and on what page helped provide cues for its recall. By contrast, when the material was typed on a continuous scroll with no pages or page numbers, recall was reduced by 25 per cent. All this relates to the context in which something is learned. Recall is easier if the context can be reconstructed as well as the actual material.

Context and Memory

Not unrelated to the above is what is known as the **encoding specificity principle**. Tulving (1983) suggests that recollection of an event occurs if and only if the properties of the trace of the event found in memory are sufficiently similar to the properties of the cue information presented at the time of retrieval. In practice this means that recall is likely to be best when the context in which learning takes place is the same as that in which testing is done. In one experiment Smith *et al.* (1978) asked participants to learn material in two very different settings. On one day they had to learn words in a windowless room with a large blackboard and no cabinets, where the experimenter was formally dressed in a jacket and tie. On another day they learned a different set of words in a tiny room with two windows with the experimeter dressed in open-necked shirt and jeans. Then on the next day they were tested on both sets of words, half of them in the windowless room with the formally dressed experimenter, the other half in the tiny but well-lit room with the casually dressed experimenter. Recall was best of material learned in the same setting, with those tested in the same context recalling an average of 13.6 words, while those tested in a different context recalled only an average of 9.1 words.

It is hard to see how this encoding specificity principle can be made to operate in practice. Clearly it is likely that formal examinations, taken in a large impersonal hall with unfamiliar invigilators, by students who have done their learning in small informal groups with teachers they know well are likely to put students at a disadvantage. Administrators should take note. Students should perhaps be encouraged not to do their final revision at home, in a bedroom, perhaps with music playing, but in a classroom which comes as near as possible to the conditions they will encounter in the exam room.

Mood Congruence and State-dependent Memory

Context refers not only to the physical context in which something is committed to memory but also to an individual's physiological context when something is learned. This can include affective states (emotional and motivational states, for instance) and also factors such as states induced by drugs or alcohol. Memory appears to be better if there is a congruence between the material to be learned and the individual's mood. This is **mood congruence**. When pleasant material has to be learned, it is best learned in a pleasant frame of mind, while someone in an unpleasant mood will be better able to learn unpleasant material. Blaney (1986) reviewed 29 cases where mood had been experimentally induced and showed that in 25 of these, mood congruence had a bearing on memory. However, it is not easy to see how this can be made to operate in a study situation.

State-dependent memory may be more relevant, though. It is suggested that what people remember is at least partly determined by the physiological state they are in. The state during encoding needs to match that during recall. However, Blaney's review of the literature, mentioned above, casts some doubt on this. A significant number of studies have failed to show evidence of state dependent memory.

Recognition of People's Faces

The section in Chapter 3 (pp. 48–53) on pattern recognition concerned ways in which we are able to recognise what we have seen before, whether this is a printed letter or word or the features of a face. This has also been discussed in connection with eyewitness testimony (pp. 121–2). A teacher in front of a classroom full of children has this problem, as has a doctor faced with a succession of patients, each of whom only visits the doctor very infrequently. Imagery can help here too. On introduction, make careful note of the person's name, repeat it out loud and create a mental image for it if at all possible. Suppose, for example, the name is Sean Miller, a mental image might be created of a windmill and the miller going about his business of grinding corn. This particular miller has a crew cut (is shorn). Then look at the features of the individual in front of you superimposing them on your 'shorn miller' (nose, eyes, ears and any other distinctive feature). If any of these features remind you of some well-known person he or she too can be incorporated into your image, probably in caricature. Similarly, if the features remind you of a friend or a relative he or she can go into the image. When you meet the individual again, the image will recur and with it the name.

Strategies which Involve Organisation

As has been seen in the sections on short term and long term memory, disconnected or random material is much harder to commit to memory than material which has a pattern to it. First, the process of breaking material into chunks is important. Remember that the capacity of short term memory is around seven, plus or minus two items (Miller, 1956). But each item can be a single letter or a digit, a group of letters or digits or a word.

As an example, let us take postal codes. BS232XG is a collection of seven letters and digits with no meaning to it. It is hard to memorise. Break it up into BS23 2XG and it immediately becomes easier, a chunk of four and a chunk of three. It becomes easier still when the pattern for postal codes is known. You understand that BS refers to Bristol. A random collection of letters and numbers has been organised into fewer and more meaningful chunks.

There is evidence that the time spent in organising material so that it connects together and is meaningful is time well spent. To some extent this organisation is spontaneous. Tulving (1962) found evidence for such spontaneous organisation. He asked participants in his study to recall the same list of words in each of 16 trials. As trials progressed, there was increasing subjective organisation. This was rather a sterile process. Not many people are asked to memorise the same list of words 16 times. A more ecologically valid study was conducted by Rubin and Olson (1980). Undergraduates were asked to list members of the staff in their faculty. There was spontaneous organisation in the way they had remembered and listed the names. Those who taught the same subjects tended to be grouped together.

Hierarchical organisation has also been shown to be effective. This is a system where items are arranged in classes. It has already been seen that there is hierarchical organisation in long term memory. It might be useful to look back to pp. 104–8. Hierarchical organisation can be visualised as a kind of family tree. At the summit are the two individuals from whom all those below are descended. Each generation becomes more numerous. In the same way, hierarchical organisation of information starts with a few broad classifications and subdivides into more specific and still more specific classes. When writing notes for this section, there are broad categories of techniques for memory improvement, imagery and organisation, for instance. Within each are more specific techniques. Under the classification of imagery there is the method of loci and under this again a specific technique for memorising items along a path you regularly travel.

Linking this discussion of organisation with the previous section on imagery, there are ways in which you might re-order your notes so as to be able to remember them more accurately.

Lovelace and Southall (1983, p. 178) showed that patterns on a page can be important for memorisation. Start with the key idea in a box in the centre of the page. Highlight it by drawing and perhaps by colour. Round it like the legs of a spider, let lines radiate on which subordinate ideas are written. Outwards from these are attached the lower and more specific items in the hierarchy. Figure 4.5 illustrates the kind of pattern which might result. Then, when you come to revise for an examination, take a blank sheet of paper and attempt to re-create the pattern.

Meaningfulness and Memorisation

The section on levels of processing (pp. 111–16) clearly contains practical ways of improving memorisation. It is evident that where material has been processed so as to focus upon its meaning, recall becomes better. After all, focusing on the meaning amounts to semantic processing and this is deep and therefore effective processing in terms of memory. Learning facts by rote is a less

FIGURE 4.5

Hierarchical Notes on Memory Improvement

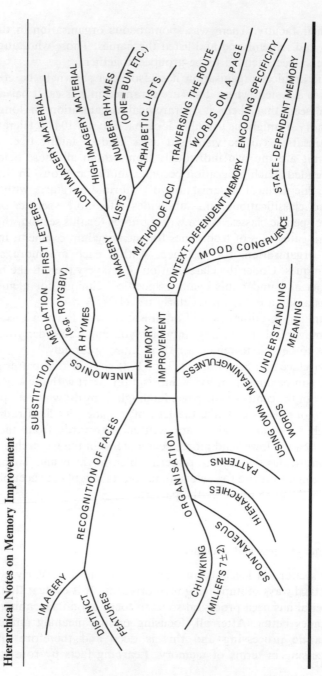

helpful way of preparing for an examination than working to tease out the meaning behind the words. If you put what you are hoping to be able to recall, into your own words you force yourself to come to terms with its meaning and so process it more deeply. Elaborating on it and trying to make it more distinctive, by, for instance, creating unusual and elaborate examples will help still further.

Mnemonic Techniques Involving Mediation

Mediation techniques involve finding a simple mediator which will help you remember something long and complex. Extra words or images are used to make material more memorable. The sentence 'Richard Of York Gained Battles In Vain' has been used by generations of school children to help them to remember the colours of the spectrum in order: Red, Orange, Yellow, Green, Blue, Indigo, Violet. The first letter of each word that you want to remember is used to make up a more meaningful sentence, preferably one which has possibilities for imagery. Alternatively, first letters can be used to form a nonsense word which is memorable through its very bizarreness. Such a word is SOHCAHTOA which still remains in my memory from schooldays. In full, it relates to trigonometrical rules for computing the angles of triangles, 'Sine is the Opposite over the Hypotenuse, Cosine is the Adjacent over the Hypotenuse, Tangent is the Opposite over the Adjacent'.

Morris (1978) showed that this technique was useful where the order of items to be remembered was important, less so when this was not the case. However, it remains one of the most popularly used techniques.

Some Other Mnemonic Techniques

Substitution

The techniques described above are useful for verbal material, but where numbers are involved it is difficult, if not impossible to use them. In these circumstances a letter can be substituted for a digit. Then mediation techniques such as the creation of words or sentences can be used. Alternatively, words may be substituted for digits, each having the same number of letters as the digit it repres-ents. For example, if you had to remember a bank cash dispenser PIN number, say 4294 then a sentence such as 'Jane is available soon' (Jane 4 letters, 'is', 2 letters, 'available' 9 letters, 'soon' 4 letters hence 4294) could be substituted. Clearly there are problems in creating and decoding such mnemonics but they are effective.

Rhymes

Rhymes are much used to help us remember. Most of us remember the number of days in each month of the year by the rhyme 'Thirty days hath September, April June and November' and so on.

These are just some of the mnemonic techniques which have been employed to enable us to use memory more effectively. The most useful way forward for individuals who want to improve their memory is to try some of them and if they seem to work for you then use them.

Self-assessment Questions

1. Describe two mnemonic techniques which involve imagery.
2. How can you make sure that you remember people's names?
3. In what ways does it help memorisation to organise the material you want to learn more carefully?
4. What is meant by mediation in memorisation?

FURTHER READING

A. D. Baddeley, *The Psychology of Memory* (New York: Basic Books, 1978).
Tony Buzan, *Use Your Head* (London: BBC Publications, 1974).
M. W. Eysenck, *A Handbook of Cognitive Psychology* (Hillsdale, N.J.: Lawrence Erlbaum, 1984).
M. Matlin, *Cognition* (Fort Worth: Holt, Rinehart & Winston, 1989).

Thinking and Language   5

At the end of this chapter you should be able to:

1. Identify various interpretations of what is meant by thinking, including Freudian, Piagetian, Gestalt and Behaviourist views.
2. Describe what are meant by 'concepts' together with some of the research into their formation.
3. Demonstrate an understanding of some of the cognitive processes involved in solving problems and factors which may facilitate or inhibit problem solving.
4. Identify various theories about the relationship between language and thought including linguistic relativity theory, Vygotsky's and Piaget's views.
5. Describe and make some evaluation of various theories about language acquisition including those of Skinner and Chomsky.
6. Compare the above critically with theories which stress the importance of social interaction in the development of language.

INTRODUCTION

In this chapter we are concerned with thinking. Problem solving and concept formation are two of the particular topics dealt with, as are various models of thinking. Additionally, the chapter is concerned with language, its acquisition, comprehension and production together with its relationship with thinking.

SECTION I   WHAT IS THINKING?

Thinking has been defined as the process involved in manipulating information, either collected through the senses or stored in memory from previous experience so as to be able to respond to the immediate situation. In this section, we shall examine various models of thinking. These include Freudian approaches, distinctions between **autistic** and **rational** thinking, Piaget's view of thinking and that of the behaviourists and the Gestalt psychologists.

Autistic and Rational Thinking

McKellar (1957) draws a distinction betwen autistic and rational thinking. Autistic thinking has no rational purpose. It is the brain's manipulation of the information available to it, from the senses or from stored material, without any particular purpose. Daydreaming is an example of autistic thinking. Rational thinking on the other hand, is logical and rational and directed towards a purpose. When you are solving the clues in a crossword puzzle you are engaging in rational thinking.

A Freudian View of Thinking

For Freud and the psychoanalysts, thinking is closely related to their view of basic human motives. For them, the basic human motive is the satisfaction of bodily needs, for air, water, food, warmth and contact with others. Where these drives are not fully satisfied, memory of them is brought into play. This memory is associated with the kind of excitation that actual food, warmth, and contact evoke. For example, a hungry infant hallucinates about food, but this hallucination is not in itself satisfying. Some of the energy released is devoted to solving the problem, to changing the environment so that the food, the warmth or the contact is obtained. This is essentially autistic thinking, driven by emotional rather than by rational processes. Freud makes a distinction between primary and secondary thought processes. While secondary thought embraces rational conscious thought of which we are normally aware, primary thought processes are normally unconscious. There seem to be three separate levels of thinking:

1. **Pre-conscious** thought, which comprises those thoughts and ideas which are not engaging our consciousness at the moment,

to which we are currently not paying attention but which nevertheless exist for us.

2. **Conscious** thought, to which we are currently paying attention and on which we are engaging our minds.
3. **Unconscious** thought, which remains inaccessible to our consciousness but which nevertheless plays a part in determining our behaviour.

Piaget's View of Thought

The building blocks of an individual's intelligence Piaget termed **schemata**. They were continually being modified or added to by contact with the environment so that the individual's adaptation to that environment becomes more complete. The process involved was one of **equilibration**. When something new manifested itself in an individual's environment his or her mind was thrown into a state of imbalance or disequilibrium. This was uncomfortable, so that there is motivation to find a new balance. This new balance occurred through **adaptation**, which took the form either of **assimilation** or else of **accommodation**. With assimilation, an object or an idea was understood in terms of the concepts or actions (schemata) which the child already possessed. With accommodation, concepts and actions were modified to fit the new situation. A fuller discussion of Piaget's theories will be found in Birch and Malim, 1988.

A Gestalt Model of Thinking

There is a classic account of a German psychologist Wolfgang Köhler, interned on the island of Teneriffe during the First World War, who set problems for a chimpanzee named Sultan. A banana was placed outside Sultan's grasp, hanging from the ceiling. There were boxes in the room which the chimpanzee could use but the problem required him to stack one box on top of another to reach the banana. At first, the animal attempted to stand on one box beneath the fruit but could not reach it. Köhler reported that Sultan sat inactive for a few minutes, then suddenly he stacked a second box on top of the first, climbed up and reached the banana. There was clearly a period of time when the elements of the problem were restructured, followed by a flash of insight as the problem snapped into focus and the solution became obvious.

Köhler saw the principle concerned here as one of **isomorphism**, the notion that the mind always attempts to restructure the elements of a problem so that the brain fields adopt **good form**, as the Gestalt psychologists described it. There is an inborn tendency within the brain to seek order out of chaos. This is in accordance with the Gestalt 'Laws of Organisation', which have already been mentioned in Chapter 3 (pp. 54–6).

A Behaviourist Model of Thinking

Behaviourists found some difficulty in explaining thinking. It did not seem to accord well with their principle that all mental processes were essentially the forming of associations between stimuli. Watson (1913) viewed thinking as sub-vocal speech. The process of thinking inevitably (as Watson saw it) involved inner language. This was a **motor theory of thought**. Some work was done with deaf mutes. It might be expected under Watson's theory that they would move their fingers more than a normal group of adults when they were thinking. They used their fingers for sign language after all. There did seem to be a higher correlation between motor activity in the fingers and thinking than in a hearing group of adults. Skinner later viewed thinking as private behaviour as opposed to overt behaviour and that it was similarly subject to stimulus control and reinforcement. In his book *Verbal Behavior* he attempted to show that both overt behaviour and thinking were controlled by operant conditioning. In overt behaviour, there was an interaction with someone else, while, with thinking, individuals are their own listeners. There is in effect an interaction with themselves.

Cognitive Approaches to Thinking

Cognitive approaches to thinking have attempted to examine the mental processes which occur during thinking. Miller *et al.* (1960) identified what they referred to as **heuristic strategies**. These were models which enabled them to simulate the way in which the mind solved problems. The complexities of a problem might be simplified by working out a series of rules of thumb. These could then be applied one at a time. Though this did not guarantee that a solution to the problem could be found, it reduced the problem to manageable proportions. A computer could then be programmed to deal with it. For example, in programming a computer to play chess, a set of instructions had to be devised such as 'check that the king is safe' or 'make sure that the queen cannot be taken'.

Newell and Simon (1972), attempted to mirror human problem-solving and behaviour in a heuristic way. To validate the models set up, they relied on individuals' verbal reports of what was going through their heads while they attempted to solve problems. In this way, computer models were constructed of how problems were solved. Within these models the program was analogous to the set of rules or instructions within which a person operated; the computer memory was analogous to the memory of the individual, and the input and output from the computer represented the problem posed and the solution found.

However, because human brains are not computers and cannot be so rigidly controlled there were difficulties, including the following:

1. It is not very useful to think of human beings as machines. Any analogy is bound to be partial only, as we do not fully understand the principles on which the human brain operates.
2. Computers, while they are very accurate and efficient calculators and solvers of logical problems, are not capable of original and creative thinking.
3. Computers are not susceptible to human emotions. They do not get tired, anxious, angry or afraid.

We shall return to a discussion of heuristic strategies at a later point.

The Structure of Knowledge

There is also quite extensive work by cognitive psychologists into the structure of knowledge. As has been mentioned in Chapter 4, generalised knowledge (p. 119) can be encoded in what have been called **schemata**. These are clusters of similar items of knowledge. They provide expectations about what should occur in relation to procedures, sequences of events and social situations and allow us to make predictions about new situations. To take an example used by Eysenck (1984), suppose you were in an unfamiliar house and needed to use the toilet. The schemata you possess about houses would lead you to rule out the living room as a place to look. However, it is just possible you might be in error and the toilet might be next to the living room!

Scripts are a particular kind of schema. They are standard sequences of events which by repetition have become predictable. You might develop a script related to going to work in the morning. You kiss your family goodbye, pick up your briefcase and a neatly furled umbrella, go out of the door and make for the station. On the way you stop at the newsagent and buy a copy of the *Guardian* before arriving at the station two minutes before the train is due to leave. This is a relatively **strong script** in that the order of events is rigidly programmed. Weak scripts do not necessarily prescribe a rigid order of events, yet the events are sufficiently stereotyped to provide expectation that they will occur.

The work on concept formation described in Section II of this chapter also comes within this category of cognitive approaches to thinking.

Self-assessment Questions

1. What is the distinction between autistic and rational thinking?
2. The Gestalt psychologists used the term 'isomorphism' to describe the way in which the brain operates. Explain briefly what the term implies.
3. In what way did behaviourists get over the difficulty they had in explaining thinking?
4. List some of the difficulties involved in computer simulation of thinking.

SECTION II   THINKING AS CONCEPT FORMATION

Introduction

When individuals form concepts, they are abstracting from something they perceive, the essential characteristics of it. They can then place it in a category alongside other items with similar characteristics, label it and respond appropriately.

Walking alongside a river, I saw in the water ripples moving about and occasionally a black head appeared. The appearance and characteristics of what I saw enabled me to place it in a category. It was clearly a mammal, not a fish, and furthermore its behaviour, size and appearance made me suppose it must have been an otter. Accordingly, my appropriate response was to tell my companions that there was an otter in the river. From descriptions, definitions and previous encounters I had formed the concept of an otter and this conceptualisation had enabled me to respond in an appropriate way. Without concepts every encounter with everything in our environment would have to be on a trial and error basis.

Concept Formation

Concept formation can be seen as rational thinking. An assortment of information, either perceived by the senses or stored in memory from previous experience, is directed towards a clear goal (the attainment of the concept) according to pre-ordained rules.

The information involved consists of **attributes** of the stimuli before us. A London bus, for instance, has various attributes; it is red, it has two decks, it is large, on wheels and carries a great many passengers. All these attributes are relevant to its conceptualisation as a London bus. It may also have attributes which are not relevant to the concept of 'London bus', which do not mark it out as a London bus particularly. It may be driven by a red-haired woman, it may have graffiti scrawled on it, but these attributes do not make it any more or any less a London bus. Attributes will also vary in their **salience**, that is, the ease with they are noticed. The colour of the bus may be a very obvious (i.e. salient) attribute, the name painted on the side is much less salient.

Concept-formation Studies

Most of the studies done by psychologists into concept formation are concerned to measure how efficiently participants learn concepts and/or what strategies they adopt to do so. Efficiency may be measured by the number of trials required to guess a concept correctly, or perhaps the number of wrong guesses before the correct one.

A classic study was that of Bruner *et al.* (1956). They devised a set of 81 cards, which varied in four ways:

1.   in their borders: the cards had one, two or three borders;
2.   in the numbers of objects: the cards had one, two or three objects on them;
3.   in the kinds of objects: the cards had one of three objects depicted on them – a square, a circle or a cross; and
4.   in the colour of the objects: the objects could be green, red or black.

The procedure for the participants was as follows. Participants worked in pairs. One of the pair (A) was invited to think of a set of attributes, for instance, all those cards with red objects on them and three borders. This constituted a concept. Then with all the cards displayed A pointed to a positive instance of the concept. The other participant (B) was then invited to select another card and ask, 'Is this one of them?' When the answer was 'No', they merely proceeded to another card, but if the answer was 'Yes', they were entitled to guess what the set of attributes (the concept) was. A measure of the ease or difficulty of attainment of a concept was the number of guesses required to reach the correct answer. The researchers also identified the strategies employed by participants.

Bruner and his colleagues identified several types of concept:

● **Conjunctive concepts**, where a card had to possess all of a set of attributes,
● **Disjunctive concepts**, where the card had only to have one or more of a number of attributes.
● **Relational concepts**, where the concept relates one attribute to another.

Here are some examples:

Conjunctive: all those cards with two borders, and green crosses.

Disjunctive: all those cards with either crosses on them, or with two borders.

Relational: all those cards with more borders than objects.

In real life you could identify a conjunctive concept as, say, a cricket ball. To be a cricket ball it needs to be round, hard, red, made of leather and to possess a seam. If it lacks any of these attributes it is not a cricket ball. A disjunctive concept might be the idea of 'out' in cricket, where one of a number things has to occur, for instance: the ball is bowled and hits the stumps; the ball hits the batsman's pads when they are in front of the wicket; the batsman hits the ball and a fielder catches it; and so on. A relational concept might be that of a quorum for a meeting, that is, where there are more people present at the meeting than a number previously fixed.

Bruner and his colleagues found that participants made use of four main strategies to identify concepts:

1. **Conservative focusing** involves focusing on the first positive instance, and then selecting a card which differed in one attribute only. With a negative response you know that that attribute is relevant. Suppose the concept was all the cards with green crosses (whatever number) and the first positive instance had two borders and one green cross, you might select a card with two borders and a single black cross. The negative response would confirm that colour was a relevant attribute. But suppose you selected a card with two borders and two green crosses (varying just the number of crosses), the positive response would indicate that the number of objects was not relevant. In this way you could test all the attributes and eventually arrive at the answer.

2. **Focus gamblers** are a much more reckless breed. They focus on the first positive example and then, when asked to select a card, choose one where two or more of the attributes are different. Suppose the concept was all cards with green crosses, and the first positive example is a card with two borders and one green cross you might select a card with two borders and two black crosses, thus varying two attributes at once. You would have lost your gamble, because the negative response would not tell you whether it was borders or colours that were relevant. On the other hand, if you selected a card with three green crosses and three borders you would get a positive response, would have won your gamble and know that both numbers and borders are irrelevant.

3. A **successive scanning** strategy starts with a hypothesis and selects cards that are relevant to that hypothesis. Take the concept of all cards with green crosses and the initial positive example of two borders and one green cross; a successive scanner would start with a hypothesis relevant to that, say, all cards with two borders, and pick a card with two black crosses and two borders. Getting a negative response, the successive scanner rejects this hypothesis and tries another, changing one attribute at a time. If, on the other hand, a card with two borders and two green crosses was selected and a positive response obtained, the hypothesis could be maintained and a guess made at the answer.

4. The least effective and most difficult strategy is that of **simultaneous scanning**. This is similar to successive scanning except that instead of scanning for one attribute at a time the simultaneous scanner attempts to remember all the attributes at once, a difficult feat of memory.

Try the following exercise to see how the procedure works.

Exercise

Link up with a friend and simulate Bruner's procedure in the following way: take a pack of playing cards, which has attributes of suits (hearts, diamonds, spades and clubs), colours, (black and red) and numbers (ace to ten and Jack, Queen, King). Ask your friend to select a concept and go through Bruner's procedure. First get her or him to point out a positive example of the concept selected, then select further cards and for each ask, 'Is that one?' Taking each of the strategies described above in turn, decide for yourself which is the most effective.

A more recent study of concept formation was that of Levine (1975) which resulted in his **theory of hypothesis testing**. The technique which he employed, the **blank trials procedure**, is as follows:

Stage one The participants are presented with a card on which there are two figures, differing in respect of four attributes, colour (black or white), size (large or small), shape (X or T) and position (left or right) and guess which figure is correct. This will, of course, be a wild guess, as there is very little to go on. The experimenter answers 'right' or 'wrong'.

Stage two The experimenter presents the participant with four new cards. Participants choose again, but this time the experimenter gives them no feedback. These are the 'blank trials'. While the participants learn nothing from these 'blank trials' the experimenter can analyse the responses and determine which attribute the participants believe to be correct.

Stage three There is a further 'feedback' trial, followed by a further four 'blank trials' and so on.

The experimenter can tell from the participants' choices on the blank trials which hypotheses they are forming. If for example, a participant has consistently chosen the right-hand position, the experimenter can infer from this that the hypothesis has been formed that the 'right' position is correct. This, then, is a way in which private thoughts can be made more public. It is, however, very slow and time-consuming.

Levine suggested that at the outset participants started with a pool of hypotheses (in the case of the example above, a possible eight hypotheses: X, T, black, white, large, small, left and right). From this pool participants would choose a smaller number of hypotheses (any number from one to eight) which seemed to them to be likely. From this smaller number of hypotheses, a **working hypothesis** would be selected. It is on this working hypothesis that the immediate response would be based. If feedback supported the chosen hypothesis, there would be no reason to change it. If on the other hand feedback did not support the hypothesis formed, the participant tried to remember as much as possible of previous trials before forming another working hypothesis. Levine suggested that people keep track of a number of other possible hypotheses, while using a current working hypothesis. If a participant had perfect memory, he or she would be able to keep track of all the hypotheses which were consistent with the feedback and would not adopt any hypothesis which had already been rejected. Given eight possible hypotheses, this marvellous person should be able to work out the answer after only three trials. Levine termed a strategy where participants keep track of as many hypotheses as possible at the same time a **global focusing strategy**. Intelligent adults seem to adopt a global focusing strategy where the task is a comparatively simple one. Where the task is more difficult or where memory skills are more limited other strategies may be adopted.

An alternative way of finding out what people are thinking when they are forming concepts involves **introspection**. The **think aloud** method involves getting participants to say out loud what they are thinking. Dominowski (1974) used this method in studying concept formation, but there are problems:

1. It seems inevitable that saying out loud what you are thinking will result in your performing the task differently. It may encourage people to use particular strategies or methods, or it may result in simply working more carefully.
2. It is uncertain to what extent we have complete access to what we are thinking. Nisbett and Wilson (1977) suggested that much of our thinking is unconscious. Participants in several studies (for example Storms and Nisbett, 1970) seemed to be entirely oblivious to the processes which determined their behaviour:

   When people are asked to report how a particular stimulus influenced a particular response, they do so not by consulting a memory of the mediating process, but by applying general causal theories about the effects of that type of stimulus on that type of response (Nisbett and Wilson, 1977, p. 248).

However, cognitive psychology has depended upon introspection. Experiments on visual illusions or on memory would be difficult without it. Ericsson and Simon (1980) have suggested some criteria to help us distinguish between valid and invalid use of introspection:

1. Reports should be obtained during and not after the performance of a task as retrospective reports are likely to be faulty.
2. Introspections about what participants are attending to or thinking are likely to be more accurate than those which involve interpretation or speculation.

3. The involvement of attention is a pre-requisite of introspection. Only information in focal attention can be verbalised.

Self-assessment Questions

1. What is meant by a concept? How does the formation of concepts assist people to react appropriately to the world around them?
2. What were the three types of concept which Bruner identified?
3. Outline in your own words the 'hypothesis testing theory' of Levine.
4. What are some of the problems inherent in using introspection to find out what people are thinking? Do Ericsson and Simon's criteria for valid use of introspection seem to you to be useful?

SECTION III   PROBLEM SOLVING

Introduction

Almost every day-to-day activity involves solving problems. They may be as simple and routine as making a cake using a recipe in a book, or as complex as finding the reason for the car not starting in the morning. It is useful to think of three elements of a problem:

1. The original situation: e.g. that of having invited people to tea and having nothing to offer them.
2. The goal situation: e.g. to have a tasty cake to offer when the visitors come.
3. The rules: e.g nothing is to be used except what is in the cupboards.

This section aims to examine problem-solving and to describe some of the research into it. This will include ways of understanding problems, methods of representing the elements of problems and strategies for solving them.

Understanding Problems

Before a problem can be solved there must be understanding of it. Understanding involves creating internally (in your head) a representation of the elements of the problem. Greeno (1977) suggests that this involves three requirements:

● Coherence
● Correspondence
● Relationship to background knowledge

For instance, in the cake-making example, quoted above, there needs to be **coherence**. The list of ingredients and the method described in the recipe need to fit together. If there is some element which does not fit, then the problem becomes difficult to solve. For instance, if the list of ingredients includes items not mentioned in the description of the method, then there is no coherence. The whole thing does not fit properly together.

There also needs to be a close **correspondence** between the internal representation and the material involved in the problem. The internal representation (the way in which we perceive the elements involved) may be inaccurate or incomplete. Instructions to beat eggs into the cake mixture will assume an internal representation of what this involves. Lack of correspondence between an individual's internal representation of this process and the assumption made in the instructions might result – to take a rather far-fetched example – in attempts to beat the eggs in, shells and all!

This is fairly closely related to the third criterion for understanding, **the relationship to background knowledge**. Instructions for baking a cake need to be in different terms for someone who is a complete novice at cooking and for someone who is already an accomplished cook. Vocabulary and concepts need to be familiar and at the right level.

Representing the Problem

Once the elements of the problem are established, it becomes necessary to find a way of representing them, a kind of shorthand which makes manipulation of the elements more manageable than it would be in the original form. There are several alternative ways of doing this:

● Symbols
● Lists

- Matrices
- Hierarchical trees
- Graphs
- Visual images

Symbols

When we learnt to solve problems in algebra, they were represented in **symbols**. To take a typical example:

Mary and Jane are friends. Mary is five years older than Jane. Five years ago Mary was twice Jane's age. How old are they now.

A common way to solve problems like this is to represent what is not known by symbols. For instance, let Mary's present age be m and Janes be j, then

$m = j + 5$ represents the first sentence of the problem.

The second sentence is represented by

$$[2(j - 5) = m - 5]$$

So we can substitute $(j + 5)$ for m in the second equation and get $2(j - 5) = j + 5 - 5$ so $j = 2j - 10$, $j = 10$, so $m = 15$. You can then check that you are right by translating back into the terms of the original problem. Mary is 15 and Jane is 10 (five years younger). Five years ago Mary was 10 and Jane was five, half her age.

The difficulty often encountered with symbols is that of oversimplification. A problem solver may misrepresent the problem when it is transformed into symbols.

Lists

This translation into symbols cannot always be done, though, and sometimes a **list** is an easier way to represent the problem. Here is the well known Orcs and Hobbits problem:

There are three Orcs and three Hobbits who want to cross a river. There is a boat which will only carry two creatures. If ever there are more Orcs than Hobbits on either bank of the river, the Orcs will immediately kill and eat the Hobbits. How can both Hobbits and Orcs get across the river without this happening?

A list could be made as follows:

Right bank	*Left bank*
3 Hobbits + 3 Orcs	none
3 Hobbits + 1 Orc	0 Hobbit + 2 Orcs
3 Hobbits + 2 Orcs	0 Hobbit + 1 Orc
3 Hobbits + 0 Orc	0 Hobbits + 3 Orcs
3 Hobbits + 1 Orc	0 Hobbit + 2 Orcs
1 Hobbit + 1 Orc	2 Hobbit + 2 Orcs
2 Hobbits + 2 Orcs	1 Hobbit + 1 Orc
0 Hobbit + 2 Orcs	3 Hobbits + 1 Orc
0 Hobbit + 3 Orcs	3 Hobbits + 0 Orcs
0 Hobbit + 1 Orc	3 Hobbit + 2 Orcs
0 Hobbit + 2 Orcs	3 Hobbits + 1 Orc
0 Hobbit + 0 Orc	3 Hobbit + 3 Orcs FINISH

This can be cumbersome and not very helpful. In this case, it does not show clearly who crosses and returns on each trip.

Matrix

One way of representing all the possible combinations is a **matrix**. This makes it easier to keep a track of the alternatives at each point. The Hobbit and Orc problem could be represented in this way:

	Boat	*Right bank*	*Left bank*	
1st crossing	2 Orcs	3H + 1O	0H + 2O	
1st return	1 Orc	3H + 2O	0H + 1O	
2nd crossing	2 Orc	3H + 0O	0H + 3O	
2nd return	1 Orc	3H + 1O	0H + 2O	
3rd crossing	2 Hobbits	1H + 1O	2H + 2O	
3rd return	1 Hobbits	2H + 1O	2H + 2O	
4th crossing	2 Hobbits	0H + 1O	3H + 2O	
4th return	1 Orc	0H + 2O	3H + 1O	
5th crossing	1 Orc	0H + 0O	3H + 3O	FINISH

This matrix makes it possible to see the results of each move as well as the move itself. Simon and Hayes (1976) found that at least 50 per cent of participants in their study used a matrix of some kind.

Hierarchical Tree

Where a problem is concerned with probabilities, then a **hierachical tree** may be the best representation of it. Take this as an example:

There is a bag full of marbles, half of which are plain glass, half are silver. The bag is shaken and a marble is drawn out. If three marbles are drawn what is the chance of getting three silver ones?

Figure 5.1 shows a hierarchical tree diagram which might make the problem easier to solve

From the diagram it is comparatively easy to see what the possible outcomes are:

silver silver silver	silver 3 glass 0
silver silver glass	silver 2 glass 1
silver glass silver	silver 2 glass 1
silver glass glass	silver 1 glass 2
glass silver silver	silver 2 glass 1
glass silver glass	silver 1 glass 2
glass glass silver	silver 1 glass 2
glass glass glass	silver 0 glass 3

FIGURE 5.1

An Example of a Hierarchical Tree

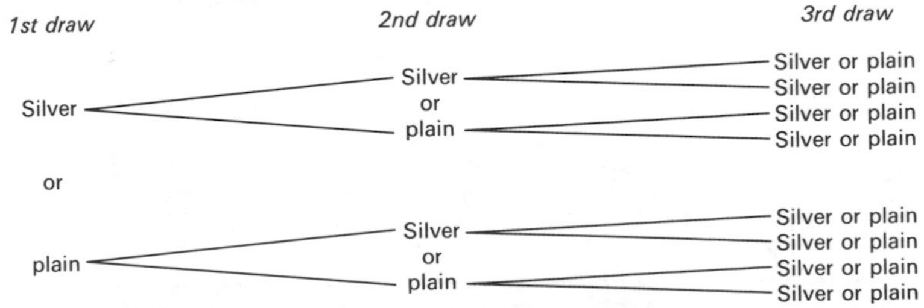

1st draw	2nd draw	3rd draw

So you can see that there is one chance in eight of obtaining three silver marbles (12.5 per cent)

Graphs

Sometimes it makes it easier if the problem is represented visually by a **graph**. The problem, described below, is perhaps best represented by a graph:

> A walker set out to climb a mountain up a steep and winding path towards the top. He climbed slowly at times, at times more quickly and sometimes he rested. At the top there was a mountain hut where he spent the night, before starting down again along the same path. Though he walked faster coming down, his speed was variable and again he rested occasionally. Prove that there must be a spot on the path which the walker will pass at the same time of day, climbing up or going down.

By plotting the time on the base axis of a graph and the height of the path on the vertical axis you can plot his progress going both ways. The lines are bound to intersect at some point as is shown in Figure 5.2.

FIGURE 5.2

A Graphic Representation of the Problem of the Walker

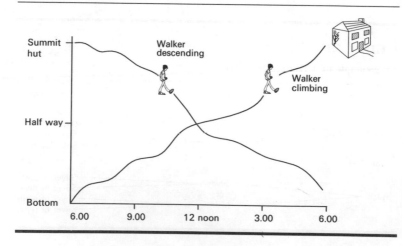

Visual Representation

It may sometimes help to use some other kind of visual representation, as may be shown in the following problem which you have probably come across before:

> There are two stations 100 km apart. At precisely the same time two trains leave, one from each station. Train A is a goods train travelling at 40 kph, train B is a passenger train which goes a little faster, at 60 kph. Overhead there is a bird flying along the track, starting from train A and not stopping until it reaches train B where it wheels around, flies back along the track to train A, where again it wheels around and returns. What distance will it need to fly at a steady 80kph before the trains meet?

A visual illustration such as that in Figure 5.3 might help solve the problem. The answer is at the end of this section.

It is clear that there is no one best way to represent a problem. Symbols, lists, matrices, hierarchical trees, graphs and visual representations can all be used. Schwartz (1971) has shown that there is a relationship between the representation of the problem and its solution. Those who did not use any particular mode of representation were found to be successful only 25 per cent of the time.

FIGURE 5.3

A Visual Representation of the Train Problem

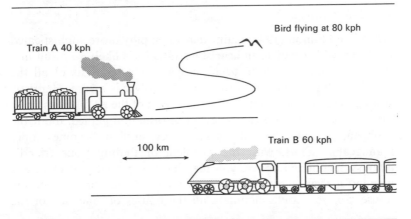

Bird flying at 80 kph

Train A 40 kph

100 km

Train B 60 kph

Strategies to Solve Problems

Once the problem has been understood and represented in one of the ways described above, strategies must be devised to arrive at a solution. These may include: (a) random search strategies; or (b) heuristic search strategies.

Random Search

A problem solver may occasionally use trial and error to solve a problem. That is to say, all kinds of possible solutions are tried but no attempt is made to be systematic or to keep records of the attempts which have been made. This is a very inefficient way to go about finding a solution to the problem which could be described as **unsystematic random search**.

Alternatively it is possible to engage in a **systematic random search**. Supposing you knew that a friend of yours lived in a particular street, an unsystematic random search might involve knocking on doors at random and asking whether he or she lived there. A systematic search would involve adopting some system to make sure no possibilities were overlooked. In the case above, this might be to knock first at number 1, then 2, then 3 and so on till the end of the street. If your friend did live in the street, you would be bound to find him or her but it might take a long time.

Heuristic Strategies

Newell and Simon (1972) claim that to employ more sophisticated strategies which they term **heuristic strategies** is likely to result in a saving of what they term **problem space**. This consists of all the possible solutions of which the problem solver is aware. Heuristic strategies involve looking at a large portion of the problem space at first, and then, by applying relevant information gained about the problem, narrow down the search area until it becomes more manageable. Thus, with the problem of finding your friend's address, mentioned above, you may have been told that there is a wonderful view across the town from the back windows of the house. So, you could eliminate all the houses on one side of the street, because none of them have that kind of a view. Your friend might also have told you that he or she lives in a bungalow, so that a further group of possible solutions to the problem can be eliminated. To take another example, suppose you have an anagram to solve while doing the crossword in the newspaper, certain combinations of letters do not occur, or occur only very rarely in English so it is not necessary to plod through all the possible combinations of letters.

Kinds of heuristic strategies include:

(a)   means-end analysis;
(b)   planning strategies; and
(c)   backwards searching.

Means-End Analysis

Another way of approaching the solution of problems is known as **means-ends analysis**. The problem is broken down into smaller elements. Each of these sub-problems can then be dealt with in the following way. First, identify the ends or goals which you want to achieve and then work on ways in which these ends can be reached. Sweller and Levine (1982) have drawn attention to the fact that means-ends analysis concentrates the solver's mind upon the essentials, the difference between the present state and the goal state.

In the Hobbits and Orcs problem, described above, there could be said to be an overall problem (to get three Hobbits and three Orcs from one side of the river to the other) and sub-problems such as the viciousness of the Orcs (they will kill Hobbits whenever they outnumber them) and the size of the boat (it will only take two at a time). Each of these sub-problems can be thought of in terms of means and ends and solutions found. The Orcs' viciousness can be neutralised by ensuring that at no time are there more Orcs than Hobbits on either side of the river. The size of the boat can be got over by making several trips and returning the boat between trips. These two sub-problems will sometimes mean that backwards moves have to be made, ferrying Orcs or Hobbits back from the left to the right side of the river.

Newell and Simon (1972) developed a computer program called General Problem Solver (GPS) based upon means-end analysis. It attempted to ape the ways in which humans tackle problems. The advantage was that it forced researchers to be clear and unambiguous about the processes used to solve problems. Computers have no tolerance of ambiguity. The program was then tested against the steps taken by humans when solving problems, to develop a theory to predict how humans solve problems.

GPS has been important in that it was the first program to simulate human behaviour. It was used to solve problems such as the Hobbits and Orcs problem, letter/number substitution problems, grammatical analysis of sentences, proofs in logic and trigonometry problems.

Planning Strategy

Other heuristic strategies include **planning strategy** which involves disregarding some aspects of a problem to make it simpler. Once the simpler problem has been solved the complications can be reintroduced. For instance, when dealing with the Hobbits and Orcs problem, a solver might disregard the viciousness of the Orcs in the first instance, and concentrate upon getting all the creatures across on a boat which would only take two at a time. Only after a solution to this simpler problem had been found would the more complicated one be tackled. Planning strategies include **analogies**, (where an earlier problem is used to compare with that currently being solved and so make it easier), and **problem isomorphs**, sets of problems with the same structures and solutions, but with different details and contexts.

Backwards Search

A further heuristic strategy is that of **backwards searching**. This involves starting at the goal and working backwards from there. Consider the game of Solitaire. This is composed of a circular board on which there are holes for 54 marbles or pegs as laid out in Figure 5.4. The player removes the centre marble and play proceeds as follows. A marble next to the vacant centre space may be

FIGURE 5.4

A Solitaire Board

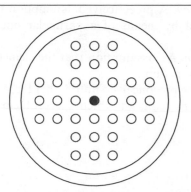

'jumped' and removed by one behind (or next to) it. The jumping and removal continues with the object of one marble finally being left in the centre space. A backwards search, starting with one marble in the centre may be one way towards solving what can be a very difficult problem.

Try this problem. A backwards search strategy may prove useful here:

Exercise

A lily on a pond doubles its size every day. If in 30 days it covers half the pond how long will it take to cover the whole pond? (The answer is at the end of this section.)

Factors which may Influence Problem Solving

Factors which may adversely affect a person's ability to solve a problem can be termed mental set. This amounts to a disinclination

of the problem solver's mind to move away from certain preconceived assumptions about the elements of the problem. This 'set'
may take several forms:

1. *Set of operation*. A preconceived assumption that the problem
    will be solved by means of a particular operation or set of
    operations.
2. *Set of function*. An assumption that the elements of a problem
    have a fixed function.
3. *Set of rule*. The preconceived notion that there are certain rules,
    within the constraints of which the problem will have to be
    solved.

Operational Set

When a person's mind assumes a fixed pattern of operation and will
not shift to an alternative pattern this can be termed **operational set**.
Luchins (1942) illustrated this with his water jar problem.

> There are three jars A, B, and C, and an unlimited supply of
> water to fill them. In a series of problems, Luchins lists the
> capacities of each of the jars, as well as the amount of water
> which has to be drawn in each case (the goal).

	A	*B*	*C*	*Goal*
1.	21	127	3	100
2.	14	46	5	22
3.	18	43	10	5
4.	7	42	6	23
5.	20	57	4	29
6.	23	49	3	20
7.	15	39	3	18

Try the problems yourself.

By the time they come to problem 6. most people have worked out
a way of solving the problems, by filling Jar B, then filling A from
it and finally filling C twice. What is left in B is the goal amount.

When they come to problem 7, they do the same thing, even though there is a much easier way of arriving at the required amount.

Functional Set

A similar phenomenon is **functional set**, sometimes termed functional fixedness. This amounts to having in your mind a fixed notion of what each element in a problem is for. The ring and peg problem desribed by Scheerer (1963) illustrates this well.

Ring and Peg Problem

Task

Participants were required to put two rings on a peg from a position two metres from the rings and the peg. They could not do this without a tool to extend their reach. When they were not actually engaged in picking up the rings and placing them on the peg they were allowed to move freely around the room and use anything they saw there. There were two sticks but neither was long enough to bridge the gap alone without joining them together. The only piece of string in the room was that by which an object was hanging from a nail on the wall. It was in clear view.

The first 16 participants (the control group) had the string hanging alone on the nail and they had no difficulty in taking it down, tying the sticks together and solving the problem. Experimental groups of participants found the string performing various functions. Group A found the string hanging things up which had no function (an out-of-date calendar, a blank piece of cardboard or a cloudy mirror). Group B found the string was hanging objects up such as a 'No Smoking' sign, a current calendar and a clear mirror. In all cases the string was tied with a square knot in plain sight above the nail.

All the group A participants succeeded in using the string to solve the problem. Of group B 56 per cent failed with the current calendar, 69% with the clear mirror and 53 per cent with the 'No Smoking' sign. In interviews afterwards, none thought they were forbidden to take down the string, but they did not think to do so.

Set of rule

Consider the following problems:

Take 6 matches and assemble them to form four equilateral congruent triangles each side of which is equal to the length of the matches.

or

Nine dots are arranged in the form of a square (as illustrated). Draw four continuous straight lines to connect them all without lifting your pencil from the paper.

●   ●   ●

●   ●   ●

●   ●   ●

Answers are at the end of this section (pp. 163–4).

When assumptions are made that a problem has to be solved within the constraints of certain rules though no such rules have been imposed it can be termed a **set of rule**. This is what may happen here. With the match problem there is no imposed constraint that the triangles must be in two dimensions. In the nine dots problem there may be an implicit constraint that you need to keep within the square.

A Question of Insight

Insight refers to a sudden flash of inspiration in relation to the solution of a problem. Gestalt psychologists suggested that the elements of a problem, which initially had seemed unrelated, suddenly come together to form coherence, a sudden cognitive reorganisation. Weisberg and Alba (1981) examined the nine dot problem described above. Participants in their experiment were each given 20 blank sheets of paper on which to attempt solutions of the problem. If they had not solved it after ten attempts they were divided into four groups:

1. A control group who were given no further help with the problem.
2. A group who were told that once they had exhausted all the possibilities within the square, they would have to go outside it.
3. A group who were also told to look outside the square but in addition were shown where to put the first line.
4. A group who were shown where to put the first two lines.

While none of the control group was successful in solving the problem, in group 2, 20 per cent were, in group 3, 60 per cent were and in group 4, 100 per cent were successful. This seems to indicate that it is not really enough simply to remove the unwarranted assumption that they had to stay within the square. Group 2 did not do spectacularly well.

Answers to Problems

The Train Problem

80km. The two trains are closing on each other at 100 kph. They will therefore take one hour to meet. In this time the bird will have flown 80 km.

Lily Pond Problem

Thirty-one days. It covered half the pond in thirty days and then during the next day doubled in size to cover the whole pond.

Match Problem

The three equilateral triangles form a pyramid. There is nothing in the problem which suggests that the answer has to be in two dimensions.

The Nine Dots Problem

There is nothing in the question which suggests that the solver has to remain within the square.

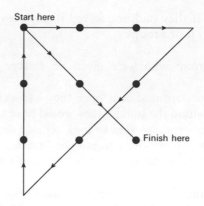

Self-assessment Questions

1. List three ways of representing a problem. What are the limitations of each?
2. Means-end analysis is an important heuristic strategy. What is meant by a heuristic strategy?
3. What is meant by 'set' in relation to problem solving? How does it relate to perceptual set, described in Chapter 3?

SECTION IV   LANGUAGE IN RELATION TO THINKING

This section is concerned with the relationship between thought and language. There are essentially four views taken on this relationship:

1. That language determines thought.
2. That thinking determines linguistic development.
3. That the two are independent of one another, but each has an influence upon intellectual development.
4. The behaviourist view that thought is internal speech.

The first of these viewpoints is represented by Whorf's **linguistic relativity** hypothesis, the second is Piaget's viewpoint and the third represents Vygotsky's view. The behaviourist view is represented by Watson.

Additionally, this section will examine the theses of Bernstein and Labov which relate to language and social class in the first case and language and race in the second.

Linguistic Relativity

Whorf (in Carroll, 1956) suggested that the language people used determined their perception of the world and consequently their thought. As evidence, they cited the language of the Hopi Indians in North America. Unlike most European languages the Hopi language has no grammatical forms, constructions or words for time. This suggests that the Hopi do not think about time in the way we do. They also had no separate words for insect, aeroplane or pilot. Is it feasible to suggest that they did not differentiate between them? Eskimos have a great many different words for snow, differentiating snow suitable for making igloos from snow suitable for sledging, for instance. Whorf suggests that this is evidence that their thinking about snow is more complex than ours is.

Evidence for Linguistic Relativity

Some support comes from a study of the Navajo Indians by Carroll and Casagrande (1958). They studied three groups of participants:

1. Those who spoke only Navajo.
2. Those who spoke Navajo and English.
3. American children of European descent who spoke nothing but English.

The form of things is very important to the Navajos and this is reflected in their language. Different verbs are used for handling long, flexible objects from those used for handling long rigid objects, for instance. American children develop object recognition in this order; size, then colour and finally form or shape. If Whorf and Sapir are right, you would predict that Navajo-speaking children would develop recognition of objects by their form at an earlier stage than American children. This is what Carroll and Casagrande found.

   The difficulty with linguistic relativity is a chicken and egg problem. There is no way of being sure which comes first, the environment or the language. Whorf and Sapir assumed that in the beginning there was language and it was language which determined the way in which people perceived and thought about things.

But it could equally well have been the other way around. The hundreds of camel-related words in Arabic or the 92 words for rice used by the Hanuxoo people of the Philippines simply reflect the nature of the worlds they live in and the things which are important to them. It is likely that language simply highlights differences in the environments of different people and provides labels to store these differences in memory.

There is also a problem which relates to the flexibility of language. It is not static, but new terms, relating perhaps to new technology or perhaps to the use of jargon, are continually being introduced. This seems to indicate that thought is the father of language rather than the other way around. If it were not so, but if thought always needed to reflect language there would be no means to introduce fresh thinking. Changes in language use would not by themselves suffice to bring about change. The spur, as in new technology, must be original thinking.

Restricted and Elaborated Codes of Language

Hess and Shipman (1965) have drawn attention to the differences in the ways in which language is used in low status and high status families. In high status (middle class) families language conveys meaning. It describes, explains and expresses feelings. In low status (working class) families language tends to be used more to give orders to the child, who is thus deprived of the same access to meaning as higher status children.

Bernstein (1961) claims that working class and middle class children use different language codes:

1. Restricted code, used by working class children is syntactically crude, has short, grammatically simple sentences, a restricted vocabulary and is context bound (that is to say, meaning depends to a high degree upon the context).
2. Elaborated code, used by middle-class children employs a larger vocabulary, more complex and flexible grammar and syntax and allows abstract thought to be expressed more easily.

This seems to point to there being a link between the kind of language used by individuals and the thought processes and intellectual development of these individuals.

Bernstein claims that the lack of an elaborated code of language is a barrier to working class children developing their full intellectual potential. Additionally, the pattern of learning in schools is based upon the use of an elaborated code. Teachers are after all generally middle class and certainly equipped with elaborated codes of language. They may not communicate adequately with some of the working class children in their charge.

It has been suggested that the terms restricted and elaborated are value-laden; that middle class language is in some way superior. This is perhaps misleading. It is likely that most people employ what Bernstein would regard as a restricted code for some of the time. There is certainly some upper-class language usage which is just as restricted. Educated people have access to an elaborated code which they can use when they need to. Some less well-educated people do not. This places them at a disadvantage intellectually.

In a similar way, researchers such as Labov (1970), Houston (1970) and Williams (1972) have studied the dialects used by black Americans. They have found them to be profoundly different from 'standard' English. Children often employ two distinct modes of speech, one for home, one for school. The school mode is not well developed and thoughts are not so easily expressed. Consequently, it has been frequently asserted that they are intellectually inferior. However, Williams (1972) developed a Black Intelligence Test, written in a dialect in which black children were more skilled. They performed much better on this test, while Genshaft and Hirt (1974) found white children performed poorly on it.

Thought as Sub-vocal Speech

A more extreme view has been taken by behaviourists and in particular by Watson (1913). His suggestion was that thinking was **sub-vocal speech**. The assumption was made that when someone attempted to solve a problem it necessarily involved some kind of inner language. When individuals struggle with a problem, especially in stressful conditions, they frequently talk to themselves. If you enter an infant classroom, there will often be a buzz evident, of children vocalising their thoughts. But this is not the same as saying that it is necessary for them to vocalise in order to think. A study carried out by Smith *et al.* (1947) would seem to indicate that it is not. Smith was given a curare derivative which paralysed him totally. He was kept alive on an artificial respirator. Sub-vocal speech was impossible. Thought should also (according to Watson's hypothesis) have been impossible. Neveretheless, he later reported that he was able to understand and think about what people were saying while he was paralysed.

The Influence of Thought upon Language

Piaget claimed that language was just one among a number of symbolic functions. Others included symbolic play and imagery. He maintained that:

> Language and thought are linked in a genetic circle ... in the last analysis, both depend upon intelligence itself, which antedates language and is independent of it (Piaget, 1968).

Piaget has taken an opposite view of the relationship between thought and language to Whorf and Sapir. For him, intellectual development comes first, and without it language is little more than meaningless babble. As an illustration of this, Sinclair-De-Zwart (1969) studied children who had acquired **conservation of volume**, (a level of intellectual development where children can appreciate that the volume of a liquid remains constant even when it is poured from a tall slender container to a short squat one). He found that they understood the meaning of words such as 'more', 'bigger', 'as much as'. Those children who had not reached the stage of conservation of volume found it hard to use such words correctly even when given specific linguistic training.

For Bruner language and thought are separate. He postulated three ways in which a child can retain and use information from the environment:

1. Through **enactive representation**, that is to say by means of physical manipulation of the environment.
2. Through **iconic representation**, that is picturing the environment mentally.
3. Through **symbolic representation**, particularly through language.

Non-linguistic thought comes first (what he terms enactive or iconic representation of the world). After language has developed, thought is amplified and accelerated in symbolic representation.

Thought and Language as Separate and Independent

Vygotsky (1962) held that language had two distinct aspects: (a) as a monitor and controller of a person's private thoughts (**inner speech**); and (b) as a means of communicating those thoughts to others (**external speech**). He believed that in infancy, thinking and language are independent. To begin with, a child's attempts to use language represent purely social speech, with no inner thought. Simultaneously, the child is developing primitive forms of thinking and reasoning, which do not involve language. Then, at about the age of two the social speech and the primitive thinking begin to come together. Words begin to act as symbols for thoughts. Vygotsky would agree with Piaget that the earliest thought is independent of language but where they part company is that Vygotsky believed that language plays an essential part in a child's intellectual development after about the age of two. Later, after about the age of seven, language and thought again separate, with language having two distinct functions: (a) internal language for the child itself as an aid to thought (**egocentric speech**); and (b) external language as a means of communicating thought to others.

Luria and Yudovich (1956) studied a pair of twins. Up to five years old they had played almost exclusively together and had developed only the most rudimentary form of language. Then they were placed in separate nursery schools and the researcher's reported as follows:

> The whole structure of the mental life of both the twins was simultaneously and sharply changed. Once they acquired an objective language system, the children were able to formulate the aims of their activity verbally and after only three months we observed the beginnings of meaningful play (Luria and Yudovich, 1956).

This seems to back up Vygotsky's view. The relationship which has been found between language and intellectual development by Bernstein in respect of social class differences, and by Labov in respect of race differences provides additional evidence that intellectual development is mediated through language.

Self-assessment Questions

1. Describe the theory of linguistic relativity. What were its weaknesses?
2. What are the essentials of Vygotsky's view of the relationship between thought and language? How convincing do you find them?
3. Does the work of Bernstein and Labov seem to you to support the notion that language determines thought?

SECTION V   LANGUAGE ACQUISITION

Introduction

Virtually all human beings learn to speak in early childhood. In general they do not have to strive to learn, nor are they specifically taught to speak. By the time they are three or four they are expressing themselves with confidence, using grammatically correct sentences. This is, by any standards, a remarkable achievement. Language involves separate systems all of which need to be mastered:

1. Phonology which involves the correct deployment of the repertory of sounds which infants have at their disposal to make up words.
2. Syntax, which relates to the set of rules for stringing sentences together. In English 'John walks in the park' is correct syntax, whereas 'in the walks John park' is not.
3. Morphology, which relates to the ways in which words change their form in accordance with the grammatical task they have to perform. For instance, a change from singular into plural in the following sentence 'The wolf roams the forest' involves changes in the morphology of 'wolf' to 'wolves' and roams to roam, 'Wolves roam the forest'.
4. Semantics, which relates to the meanings of words. Some words will not go with others because their meanings are incompatible. You can talk about 'green grass' but you cannot refer to 'green truth', (at least, I do not think you can!). There are on the other hand words which might be compatible in both cases, 'the whole truth' and 'the whole grass'.

There is little agreement on how it is achieved. In this section we shall discuss:

1. Skinner's explanation of language as **verbal behaviour**, which represents the behaviourists' answer to the problem.
2. Chomsky's view of language as an **innate, species-specific** ability in humans.
3. A third view of language acquisition which can best be described as **interactionist**, an explanation of language which places it in the context of the child, his or her environment and the need to communicate.

A Behaviourist Interpretation of Language

The behaviourists interpretation of how language is acquired, rests on the assumption of a 'tabula rasa'. That is to say, we are born with a clean slate. There is no innate endowment. All behaviour (and this includes language behaviour) is learned. The best-known exponent of this view is Skinner (1957).

In his view, a child's utterances amount to little more than a random babble of sounds to begin with. These sounds, which a child happens to produce may be reinforced (in which case they will tend to recur) or else they will not be reinforced and so will not recur. At the outset, there has to be some need to communicate, equivalent to the need for food which motivates animals to do what is necessary to find it. Skinner divides **verbal behaviour**, as he terms it, into three: **mands**, **tacts** and **echoic responses**:

1. A mand is the response to a need stimulus such as being thirsty which might prompt the child to utter something approximating to 'DRINK'. If this mand is a reasonably close approximation, then reinforcement may occur and the child may obtain a drink. This may be accompanied by the adult's repetition (correctly) of the word.
2. A tact, on the other hand, is the response to a stimulus which arouses curiosity in the child, something in his or her environment. The child might utter something approximating to 'CAT', indicating the animal lying by the fire. The reinforcement comes with the adult responding something like, 'Yes, darling: cat'.

3. Skinner also makes reference to what he calls **echoic responses** where children imitate 'tacts' and receive reinforcement from their caregivers for this imitation. This reinforcement will make it more likely that the child will use the word again.

This is entirely dependent on the external environment but there seem to be several serious difficulties:

1. Nearly all children manage to learn language and yet their environments vary enormously.
2. There seems to be roughly the same sequence as well as the same speed of learning language, regardless of the external environment.
3. From a very early stage children seem to be able to understand the way in which sounds are broken up into words and phrases. This seems to pre-suppose some natural pre-disposition towards features of language such as stress patterns.
4. It is difficult to explain why children produce language forms which they will not have heard, 'Me runned home' for instance.
5. Children have been found to make consistent errors, such as adding '-ed' to any verb to make the past tense ('goed' for 'went', or 'shaked' for 'shook'). They seem to be very good at making the wrong generalisations.
6. There is evidence that parents will correct their children's utterances more for meaning than for grammatical accuracy. Brown *et al.* (1969) found that mothers responded to the 'truth value' of their childrens utterances rather than grammatical correctness or complexity. Braine (1971) and Tizard (1972) have found that efforts to correct grammar and pronunciation seem to have little effect. Slobin (1973) even found that parents often reinforce incorrect grammar. They are too involved with interacting with the child to worry about grammatical correctness.

Skinner only detailed the very simplest of utterances. Most forms of verbal behaviour are not of this kind, but take the form of someone saying something and someone else replying. These utterances, which Skinner referred to as **intra-verbal responses**, he found much more difficult to explain in terms of stimulus-response and reinforcement. For these reasons, Skinner's account does not seem to be an adequate explanation for the phenomenon of language acquisition.

A Rationalist Explanation

The rationalist view is represented by Chomsky who regards capacity for language as a genetic endowment. A child is born with a theory about the structure of language. Consequently, it does not require more than a few instances to enable children to work out how a language is organised. This genetic endowment is termed by McNeill (1966) a **language acquisition device (LAD)**. The LAD predisposes the child to recognise grammatical structures such as noun phrases and verb phrases. **Linguistic universals** such as nouns, adjectives and verbs exist in all languages and it is these linguistic universals which the child is pre-disposed to recognise.

Chomsky distinguished between the **surface structure** of what is spoken and the **deep structure**. The surface structure represents the actual words and phrases which make up the sentence, while the deep structure corresponds more or less to the meaning of the sentence. The understanding of how to transform this deep structure into the surface structure is what he terms **transformational grammar**.

Here are three sets of examples which make this clearer:

1. Take these two sentences:

   John was chased by a bull

   A bull chased John

The surface structure of these two sentences is very different. Every word has a different position, the form of the verb has changed and the subject is different in each case. Yet the deep meaning of the two sentences is the same.

2. Now look at these sentences:

   Some children are easy to please
   Some children are anxious to please

One word only has changed but the deep meaning is quite different. In the first instance the children are the object who are easily pleased, in the second they are the active subject, wanting to please.

3.   Now read this sentence:

They are eating apples

You can either stress the word 'eating', meaning that the apples are good to eat, or put the stress more on the word 'apples', implying that these people are eating apples rather than some other fruit. The surface structure remains the same in either case, though the deep structure is different.

Chomsky maintained that the way in which people understand language is to transform the surface structure of what they hear into its **kernel** form. A similar transformation takes place when speech is produced, but in this case it is from deep to surface structure. In general, Chomsky suggested that the more transformations which have to occur between surface and deep structure the more difficult the resulting sentence is. Transformations may be between active and passive forms, positive and negative forms or perhaps between question and statement forms. So, 'The bull chased John' represents the simplest form, nearest to the kernel, 'John was chased by the bull' is more difficult and 'Wasn't John chased by the bull?' more difficult still. It has no fewer than three transformations, active to passive, positive to negative and statement to question.

The capacity which an individual has for learning language consists of the capacity to acquire and apply sets of rules. These are of several different kinds.

1. **Syntactical rules**.   These are rules by which a sentence may be strung together. For instance, while the sentence 'the bull chased John' is perfectly correct, 'chased the bull John' is not. Chomsky (1957) made the point that nearly all utterances are novel in the sense that they have not been uttered before. They cannot therefore have been learned in the way that Skinner suggests. Capacity to apply these **syntactical rules** Chomsky referred to as **competence**. Speakers do, of course, utter ungrammatical sentences sometimes and this is especially true of children learning language. These are

(according to Chomsky) **errors in performance** which do not affect the underlying competence.

Braine (1963) in his research aimed to apply these ideas of Chomsky's to the way in which children use syntactical rules in their early utterances. Analysing his young son's utterances in some detail, he came to the conclusion that there were two classes of words:

(a) **Pivot words** which occurred in a particular position in an utterance. Some would always occur first in an utterance; others always second. These included such words as 'all gone, bye bye, big, more, pretty, my, see, night night, hi'.

(b) **Open words** which might occur equally well in first or second position, such as 'boy, sock, boat, fan, milk, plane, shoe, Mummy, Daddy, hot.'

So the utterances of infants will include combinations of pivot and open words, such as 'all gone milk', 'bye bye Daddy'.

2. **Semantic rules**. These are rules concerned with meaning. Clearly, there are words which may be put together to form a sentence in a perfectly grammatical way and yet mean nothing. Chomsky quotes an example.

Colourless green ideas sleep furiously.

Lenneberg (1967) also claims that language is an innate capacity, species-specific to humans. Almost all humans acquire language irrespective of IQ. His research with Down's syndrome children has suggested that while the rate of both motor and language development is slower, there is a very similar correlation between motor and language development for all children. This seems to suggest that language acquisition is to an extent a matter of maturation. The years before puberty he regards as a critical period for language development. This perhaps explains why so-called 'wild' children – those thought to have been brought up by wild animals – do not acquire language. In many instances they have passed the critical period before having contact with humans.

Bloom (1970), researching childhood utterances, maintained that the meaning of the utterance must be taken into account. One of the children she studied produced the utterance 'Mummy sock' in two different contexts, one where her mother was putting a sock on the child's foot, the other while picking up her mother's sock. The intended meanings are very different. Brown (1973) drew up a list of **semantic relations**, the intended meanings a child might want to convey, such as:

Relation	*Example*
Agent-action	Daddy mend
Action-object	drink milk
Agent-object	Mummy clothes
Action location	hide cupboard
Object location	sock cupboard
Possessor possessed	Rachel ball
Attribute object	big dog
Demonstrative object	this house

While this accounts for the inclusion of meaning into an infant's utterances, it does not really explain how a child makes an appropriate utterance to convey its meaning in a particular context. For this, it is necessary to consider interactions between children and adults.

More general critcisms of Chomsky's view of language acquisition include the following:

1. Language learning is not just about learning the structures or the rules, but also about learning the social functions of language. You cannnot divorce language from the context in which it is used. Bruner (1983) saw language as 'a by-product (and a vehicle) of culture transmission'.
2. It ignores the fact that parents modify and simplify their language to structure the language input for their children. Chomsky is suggesting that the environment is inadequate for language learning.
3. It suggests that children's linguistic achievements are proceeding quite separately from their intellectual development, that learning to talk about something is separate from forming a concept of it.

An Interactionist Approach to Language

Proto-conversations

Before babies reach the stage of making any meaningful utterance they have begun to communicate. Trevarthen (1974) and Condon and Sander (1974) have researched what they term **proto-conversations**. These referred to early mouth movements observed during interactions. Babies appeared to synchronise their movements with the rhythms of adult speech.

Kaye and Brazelton (1971) studied the behaviour of babies during feeding sessions. They discovered that there seems to be an interrelationship between the mother's 'jiggling' of her baby and the pattern of bursts and pauses in sucking. The jiggling would seem to stop a baby sucking and the baby would begin a new burst of sucking when the jiggling stopped. Newson (1974) interpreted these findings as the child acquiring concepts by the mother 'marking' certain events in the interaction with her baby by her responses. She marks a pause in sucking by jiggling so that the baby comes to acquire the concept of a pause. Other events too, burps, sneezes and the rest are also marked by a response on the mother's part. Newson saw it as important that the marking was an experience, shared by both participants, which he termed **intersubjectivity**. The mother is setting a framework within which the child can develop intentions, meanings and subsequently language.

Bruner (1975, 1983) argues that these adult-child interactions help the child to discover the social function of communication. Important routines or rituals develop in interactions between adults and children. Examples include games such as 'peek a boo' or 'ride a cock horse' and home-made rituals at feeding and bath time. Parent and child develop predictable roles to act out and later on predictable utterances to accompany the action. Bruner refers to this as a **language acquisition support system** (LASS). The emphasis in looking at how language is acquired has moved from Skinner's mechanistic conditioning processes and Chomsky's innate linguistic detectors to how children try to understand and make themselves understood alongside adults who are also trying to understand and make themselves understood. The emphasis is upon function rather than form (grammar, syntax and semantics) and upon the culture in which the language is used.

Pragmatics

After these proto-conversations a child begins to learn words which help understanding in interactions between adult and child. **Pragmatics** refers to the acquisition of a set of rules guiding the use of different utterances to get what they want and obtain new information. Pragmatic utterances seem to fall into three categories:

1. Request or demand e.g 'Give me a drink'.
2. Question e.g 'Where doggy gone?'
3. Statement e.g. 'Food all gone'.

Nelson (1981) suggested that children fall into two groups according to the way in which they use pragmatic rules:

1. Referential children: these children's early vocabulary consists of a high proportion of names of objects, together with some verbs, proper names and adjectives.
2. Expressive children: these are children whose early vocabulary contains a large number of social utterances, such as 'Stop it', 'I want it'.

These **expressive children** seem to use language more often for social purposes than the referential children. **Referential children** use language more for cognitive purposes, such as making statements.

Conclusion

By the age of about three most children seem to have mastered many language skills. These include:

1. The rules of syntax which govern the types of word order which are acceptable and those that arc not.
2. Semantic rules governing the ways in which words can be put together to make sense.
3. Pragmatics which embody the rules necessary to carry on a conversation.

Self-assessment Questions

1. What did Skinner mean by 'mands', 'tacts' and echoic responses? What seem to you to be the main difficulties with his interpretation of how language is learned?
2. What did Chomsky mean by the term transformational grammar? Does there seem to be evidence to support him?
3. What is meant by LAD? Does it seem reasonable to you that such a device exists innately?
4. Outline the origins of pragmatics in the proto-conversations of babies.

FURTHER READING

A. Birch and T. Malim (for further discussion of language acquisition), *Developmental Psychology* (Basingstoke: Macmillan, 1988).

J. S. Bruner *Child's Talk: Learning to Use Language* (Oxford: Oxford University Press, 1983).

M. Matlin, *Cognition* (Fort Worth: Holt, Rinehart & Winston, 1989).

A. Newell and H. A. Simon, *Human Problem Solving* (Englewood Cliffs: Prentice Hall, 1972).

M. W. Eysenck, 1984 *A Handbook of Cognitive Psychology* (chapter on Language and Thought) (Hillsdale, N.J.: Lawrence Erlbaum, 1984).

Bibliography

Allport, D. A. (1955) *Becoming* (Yale University Press).

Allport, D. A, B. Antonis and P. Reynolds (1972) 'On the division of attention: A disproof of the single channel hypothesis', *Quarterly Journal of Experimental Psychology*, 24, 225–35.

Atkinson, R. C. and M. R. Raugh (1975) 'An application of the mnemonic keyword method to the learning of a Russian vocabulary', *Journal of Experimental Psychology: Human Learning and Memory*, 104, 126–33.

Atkinson, R. C. and R. M. Shiffrin (1968) 'Human memory: A proposed system and its control processes', in K. W. Spence and J. T. Spence (eds), *The Psychology of Learning and Motivation: Advances in Research and Theory*, vol. 2 (New York: Academic Press).

Baddeley, A. D. (1981) 'Reading and working memory', *Bulletin of the British Psychological Society*, 35, 414–7.

Baddeley, A. D. (1984) 'The fractionation of human memory,' *Psychological Medicine*, 14, 259–64.

Baddeley, A. D. and G. Hitch (1974) 'Working Memory', in G. H. Bower (ed.) *Psychology of Learning and Motivation*, Vol. 8 (London: Academic Press).

Baddeley, A. D. and V. J. Lewis (1981) 'The inner active processes in reading: The inner voice, the inner ear and the inner eye', in A. M. Lesgold and C. A Perfetti (eds), *Interactive Processes in Reading* (Hillsdale, N.J.: Lawrence Erlbaum).

Barclay, C. R. (1986) 'Schematization of autobiographical memory', in *Autobiographical Memory* (New York: Cambridge University Press).

Barrera, M. and D. Maurer (1981) 'Perception of facial expressions by the three-month-old', *Child Development*, 52, 203–6.

Bartlett, F. C. (1932) *Remembering: A Study in Experimental and Social Psychology* (Cambridge: Cambridge University Press).

Bellezza, F. S. (1983) 'The spatial arrangement mnemonic', *Journal of Educational Psychology*, 75, 830–7.

Bellezza, F. S. (1986) 'A mnemonic based on arranging words in visual patterns', *Journal of Educational Psychology*, 78, 217–24.

Bernstein, B. (1961) 'Social structure, language and learning', *Educational Research*, June 1961.

Biederman, I. (1987) 'Recognition by components: A theory of human image understanding' *Psychological Review*, 94, 115–17.

Bitterman, M. E. and C. W. Kniffin (1953) 'Manifest anxiety and perceptual defense', *Journal of Abnormal and Social Psychology*, 48, 248–52.

Birch, A. and T. Malim (1988) *Development Psychology: From Infancy to Adulthood* (Basingstoke: Macmillan).

Blakemore, C. and C. R. Cooper (1970) 'The development of the brain depends on the visual environment', *Nature*, 228, 477–8.

Blaney, P. H. (1986) 'Affect and memory: A review', *Psychological Bulletin*, 99, 229–46.

Bloom, L. (1970) *Language Development: Form and Function in Emerging Grammars* (Cambridge, Mass: MIT Press).

Bousfield, W. A. (1953) 'The occurrence of clustering in the recall of randomly arranged associates', *Journal of General Psychology*, 49, 229–40.

Bower, G. H. (1970) 'Analysis of a mnemonic device', *American Scientist*, 58, 496–510.

Bower, G. H. (1972) 'Mental imagery and associative learning', in L. Gregg (ed.), *Cognition in Learning and Memory* (New York: Wiley).

Bower, G. H., M. C. Clark, A. M. Lesgold and D. Winzenz (1969) 'Hierarchical retrieval schemes in recall of categorized word lists', *Journal of Verbal Learning and Verbal Behaviour*, 8, 323–43.

Bower, T. G. R. (1965) 'Stimulus variables determining space perception in infants', *Science*, 149, 88–9.

Bower T. G. R. (1982) *Development in Infancy* 2nd edition, (San Fransisco: W. H. Freeman).

Bower, T. G. R., J. M. Broughton and M. K. Moore, (1970) 'Infant responses to approaching objects: An indicator of responses to distal variables', *Perception and Psychophysics*, 9, 193–6.

Braine, M. (1963) 'On learning the grammatical order of words', *Psychological Review*, 70, 115–20.

Braine, M. D. S. (1971) 'On two types of models of the internalization of grammar', in D. I. Slobin (ed.), *The Ontogenesis of Grammar* (New York: Academic Press).

Briand, K. A. and R. M. Klein (1987) 'Is Posner's "beam" the same as Treisman's "glue"? On the relation beween visual orienting and feature integration theory', *Journal of Experimental Psychology: Human Perception and Performance*, 13, 228–41.

Broadbent, D. E. (1958) *Perception and Communication* (Oxford: Pergamon).

Broadbent, D. E. (1977) 'Levels, hierarchies and the locus of control', *Quartely Journal of Experimental Psychology*, 29, 181–201.

Brown, G. D. A. (1990) 'Cognitive science and its relation to psychology' *The Psychologist*, August 1990, pp. 339–43.

Brown R., C. B. Cazden and U. Bellugi (1969) 'The child's grammar from I to III', in J. P. Hill (ed.) *Minnesota Symposium on Child Psychology*, Vol. 2 (Minneapolis: University of Minnesota Press).

Brown, R. and J. Kulik (1977) 'Flashbulb memories', *Cognition*, 5, 73–99.

Bruner, J. S. (1975) 'From communication to language: A psychological perspective', *Cognition*, 3, 225–87.

Bruner, J. S., J. J. Goodnow and G. A. Austin (1956) *A Study of Thinking* (New York: Wiley).

Bruner, J. S and A. L. Minturn (1955) 'Perceptual identification and perceptual organisation', *Journal of General Psychology*, 53, 21–8.

Bruner, J. S. and L. Postman (1949) 'On the perception of incongruity: A paradigm', *Journal of Personality*, 18, 206–23.

Brunswik, E. (1956) *Perception and Representative Design of Psychological Experiments* (University of California Press).

Bull, B. L. and M. C. Wittrock (1973) 'Imagery in the learning of verbal definitions', *British Journal of Educational Psychology*, 43, 289–93.

Carroll, J. B (1956) (ed.), *Language, Thought and Reality: Selected Writings of Benjamin Lee Whorf* (New York: MIT Press and Wiley).

Carroll, J. B and J. B. Casagrande (1958) 'The function of language classifications in behaviour', in E. E. Maccoby, T. M. Newcombe and E. L. Hartley (eds), *Readings in Social Psychology* (New York: Holt, Rinehart & Winston).

Cherry, E. C. (1953) 'Some experiments on the recognition of speech with one or two ears', *Journal of the Acoustical Society of America*, 25, 975–9.

Chomsky, N. A. (1957) 'Review of Skinner's "Verbal Behaviour"', *Language*, 35, 26–58.

Chomsky, N. A. (1968) 'Language in the mind' in Cashdan *et al.* (eds), *Language in Education: A source book*, prepared by the Language and Learning Course Team at the Open University (London: Routledge & Kegan Paul).

Cole, M. and S. Scribner (1974) *Culture and Thought* (New York: Wiley).

Collins, A. M. and M. R. Quillian (1969) 'Retrieval time from semantic memory', *Journal of Verbal Learning and Verbal Behaviour*, 8, 240–8.

Collins, A. M and E. F. Loftus (1975) 'Spreading-activation theory of semantic memory', *Psychological Review*, 82, 407–28.

Condon, W. S. and L. W. Sander (1974) 'Neonate movement is synchronised with adult speech: Interactional participation and language acquisition', *Science*, 183, 99–101.

Conrad C. (1964) 'Acoustic confusion in immediate memory', *British Journal of Psychology*, 55, 75–84.

Coren S. and J. S. Girgus (1978) *Seeing is Deceiving: The Psychology of Visual Illusions* (Hillsdale, N.J.: Lawrence Erlbaum).

Cowan, N. (1984) 'On short and long auditory stores', *Psychological Bulletin*, 90, 218–44.

Craik, F. I. M. and R. S. Lockhart (1972) 'Levels of processing: A framework for memory research', *Journal of Verbal Learning and Verbal Behaviour*, 11, 671–84.

Craik, F. I. M. and R. S. Lockhart (1986) 'CHARM is not enough: comments on Eich's model of cued recall', *Psychological Review*, 93, 360–4.

Craik, F. I. M. and E. Tulving (1975) 'Depth of processing and the retention of words in episodic memory,' *Journal of Experimental Psychology: General*, 104, 268–94.

Crowder, R. G. (1982) 'Decay of auditory memory in vowel discrimination', *Journal of Experimental Psychology: Learning Memory and Cognition*, 8, 153–62.

Darwin, C. J., M. T. Turvey and R. G. Crowder (1972) 'An auditory analogue of the Sperling partial report procedure: Evidence for brief auditory storage', *Cognitive Psychology*, 3, 255–67.

Day, R. H. (1980) 'Visual Illusions', in M. A. Jeeves (ed.), *Psychology Survey No.3* (London: Allen & Unwin).

Den Heyer, K. and B. Barrett (1971) 'Selected loss of visual and verbal information in short term memory by means of visual and verbal interpolated tasks', *Psychonomic Science*, 25, 100–2.

Deregowski, J. B. (1968) 'Difficulties in pictorial depth perception in Africa', *British Journal of Psychology*, 59, 195–204.

de Valois R. L., I. Abramov and G. H. Jacobs (1966) 'Analysis of response patterns in LGN cells', *Journal of the Optical Society of America*, 56, 966–7.

Deutsch J. A. and D. Deutsch (1963) 'Attention: some theoretical considerations', *Psychological Review*, 70, 80–90.

Dominowski, R. L. (1977) 'Reasoning', *Interamerican Journal of Psychology*, 11, 68–70.

D'Ydewalle G., P. Delhaye and L. Goessens (1985) 'Structural, semantic and self-referencing processing of pictorial advertisements,' *Human Learning*, 4, 29–38.

Ebbinghaus, H. (1885) *Memory: a Contribution to Experimental Psychology*, trans. H. A Ruger and C. F. Bussenius (1913) (New York: New York Teachers' College, Columbia University).

Elias, C. S. and C. A.Perfetti (1973) 'Encoding task and recognition memory: The importance of semantic coding' *Journal of Experimental Psychology*, 99, 151–7.

Ericsson, K. A. and H. A. Simon (1980) 'Verbal reports as data', *Psychological Review*, 87, 215–51.

Evans, J. St. B. T. (1983) *Thinking and Reasoning: Psychological Approaches* (London: Routledge & Kegan Paul).

Ewart, P. H. (1930) 'A study of the effect of inverted retinal stimulation upon spatially co-ordinated behaviour', *Genetic Psychology Monographs*, 7, 177–366.

Eysenck, M. W. (1978) 'Verbal remembering,' in B. M. Foss (ed.), *Psychological Survey No.1* (London: Allen & Unwin).

Eysenck, M. W. (1984) *A Handbook of Cognitive Psychology* (Hillsdale, N.J.: Lawrence Erlbaum).

Fantz, R. L. (1961) 'The origin of form perception', *Scientific American*, 204 (5), 66–72.

Fisher, (1984) 'Central capacity limits in consistent mapping, visual search tasks: Four channels or more?' *Cognitive Psychology*, 16, 449–84.

Fiske, A. D. and W. Schneider (1984) 'Memory as a function of attention, level of processing and automatization', *Journal of Experimental Psychology: Learning, Memory and Cognition*, 10, 181–7.

Franks, J. J. and J. D. Bransford (1971) 'Abstraction of visual patterns', *Journal of Experimental Psychology*, 90, 65–74.

Garner, W. R. (1979) 'Letter discrimination and identification' in A. D. Pick (ed.) *Perception and its Development: A tribute to Eleanor J. Gibson* (Hillsdale, N.J.: Lawrence Erlbaum).

Gibson, E. J. (1969) *Principles of Perceptual Learning and Development* (New York: Prentice Hall).

Gibson, E. J. and R. D. Walk (1960) 'The visual cliff', *Scientific American*, April 1960.

Gibson, J. J. (1986) *The Ecological Approach to Visual Perception* (Hillsdale, N.J.: Lawrence Erlbaum).

Gilchrist, J. C. and L. S. Nesberg (1952) 'Need and perceptual change in need-related objects', *Journal of Experimental Psychology*, 44, 369.

Gilinsky, A. S. (1955) 'The effects of attitude on the judgement of size', *American Journal of Psychology*, 68, 173–92.

Gombrich, E. H. (1960) *Art and Illusion* (Oxford: Phaidon Press).

Gray, D. R. and A. A. Wedderburn (1960) 'Grouping strategies with simultaneous stimuli', *Quarterly Journal of Experimental Psychology*, 12, 180–4.

Greene, E., M. S. Flynn and E. F. Loftus (1982) 'Inducing resistance of misleading information', *Journal of Verbal Learning and Verbal Behaviour*, 21, 207–19.

Gregory, R. L. (1966) *Eye and Brain* (London: Weidenfeld & Nicolson).

Gregory, R. L. (1968) 'On how so little information controls so much behaviour', in C. H. Waddington (ed.), *Towards a Theoretical Biology* (Edinburgh: Churchill-Livingstone).

Gregory, R. L. (1970) *The Intelligent Eye* (London: Weidenfeld & Nicolson).

Gregory, R. L. (1972) 'Cognitive contours', *Nature*, 238, 51–2.

Gregory, R. L and J. Wallace (1963) *Recovery from Early Blindness* (Cambridge: Heffer).

Groninger, L. D (1971) 'Mnemonic imagery and forgetting', *Psychonomic Science*, 23, 161–3.

Haber, R. N. (1983a) 'The impending demise of the icon: A critique of the concept of iconic storage in visual information processing', *Behavioural and Brain Sciences*, 6, 1–11.

Haber, R. N. (1983b) 'The icon is really dead', *Behavioural and Brain Sciences*, 6, 43–55.

Haber, R. N. (1985) 'An icon can have no worth in the real world: Comments on Loftus, Johnson and Shinamura's "How much is an icon worth?"', *Journal of Experimental Psychology: Human Perception and Performance*, 11, 374–8.

Haider, M., P. Spong and D. Linsley (1964) 'Attention, vigilance, and evoked cortical potential in humans', *Science*, 145, 180–2.

Hardy, G. R. and D. L. Legge (1968) 'Cross modal induction changes in sensory thresholds', *Quarterly Journal of Experimental Psychology*, 20, 20–9.

Harris, J. E. (1984) 'Remembering to do things: A forgotten topic', in J. E. Harris and P. E. Morris (eds), *Everyday Memory, Actions and Absent-mindedness* (London: Academic Press).

Harris, P. L. (1983) 'Infant cognition' in P. Mussen (ed.), *Handbook of Child Psychology, Vol. II* (New York: Wiley).

Hearnshaw, L. S. (1987) *The Shaping of Modern Psychology* (London: Routledge & Kegan Paul).

Hebb, D. O. (1949) *The Organisation of Behaviour* (New York: Wiley).

Held, R. and A. Hein (1963) 'Movement-produced stimulation in the development of visually guided behaviour', *Journal of Comparative and Physiological Psychology*, 56, 607–13.

Hess, R. D. and V. Shipman (1965) 'Early experience and the socialization of cognitive modes in children', *Child Development*, 36, 860–86.

Hitch, G. J. (1980) 'Developing the concept of working memory', in G. Claxton (ed.) *Cognitive Psychology: New Directions* (London: Routledge & Kegan Paul).

Hitch, G. J. and A. D. Baddeley (1976) 'Verbal reasoning and working memory', *Quarterly Journal of Experimental Psychology*, 28, 603–21.

Howes, D. H. and R. L. Solomon (1951), 'Visual duration threshold as a function of word probability', *Journal of Experimental Psychology*, 41, 401–10.

Hubel, D. H. (1982) 'Exploration of the primary visual cortex, 1955–78', *Nature*, 299, 515–24.

Hubel, D. H and T. N. Wiesel (1962) 'Receptive fields in the striate cortex of young visually inexperienced kittens', *Journal of Neurophysiology*, 26, p. 994.

Hubel, D. H. and T. N. Wiesel (1965) 'Receptive fields of single neurons in two non-striate visual areas, 18 and 19 of the cat', *Journal of Neurophysiology*, 28, 229–89.

Hubel, D. H. and T. N. Wiesel (1979) 'Brain mechanisms and vision', *Scientific American*, 241 (3), 150–62.

Johnson, M. K. and L. Hasher (1987) 'Human learning and memory', *Annual Review of Psychology*, 38, 631–68.

Johnston, W. A. and S. P. Heinz (1978) 'Flexibility and capacity demands of attention', *Journal of Experimental Psychology: General*, 107, 420–35.

Johnston, W. A. and J. Wilson (1980) 'Perceptual processing of non-targets in an attention task', *Memory and Cognition*, 8, 372–7.

Jolicoeur, P. and M. J. Landau (1984) 'Effects of orientation on the identification of simple visual patterns,' *Canadian Journal of Psychology*, 38, 80–93.

Kahneman, D. (1973) *Attention and Effort* (Englewood Cliffs: Prentice Hall).

Kaye, K. and T. B. Brazelton (1971) 'Mother-infant interaction in the organisation of sucking', Paper delivered to Society for Research into Child Development, Minneapolis.

Kohler, I. (1964) 'The formation and transformation of the visual world', *Psychological Issues*, 3, 28–46 and 366–79.

Labov, W. (1970) *Language in the Inner City* (Philadelphia: University of Pennsylvania Press).

Labov, W. (1973) 'The boundaries of words and their meanings', in C. J. Bailey and R. Shuy (eds), *New Ways of Analysing Variation in English* (Washington: Georgetown University Press).

Lenneberg, E. H. (1967) *The Biological Foundations of Language*, New York, Wiley.

Levine, M. A. (1975) *A Cognitive Theory of Learning* (Hillsdale, N.J.: Lawrence Erlbaum).

Lindsay, P. H. and D. A. Norman (1972) *Human Information Processing: An Introduction to Psychology* (New York: Academic Press).

Linton, M. (1982) 'Transformations of memory in everyday life', in U. Neisser (ed.) *Memory Observed: Remembering in Natural Contexts* (San Francisco: Freeman).

Linton, M. (1986) 'Ways of searching and the contents of memory', in D. C. Rubin (ed.) *Autobiographical Memory* (New York: Cambridge University Press).

Loftus, E. F. and D. C. Fathi (1985) 'Retrieving multiple autobiographical memories', *Social Cognition*, 3, 280–95.

Loftus, E. F and J. C. Palmer (1974) 'Reconstruction of automobile destruction: An example of the interaction between language and memory', *Journal of Verbal Learning and Verbal Memory*, 13, 585–9.

Loftus, E. F., D. G. Miller and H. J. Burns (1978) 'Semantic integration of verbal information into visual memory', *Journal of Experimental Psychology: Human Learning and Memory*, 4, 19–31.

Loftus, E. F., C. A. Johnson and A. P. Shinamura (1985) 'How much is an icon worth?', *Journal of Experimental Psychology: Human Perception and Performance*, 11, 1–13.

Lovelace, E. A. and S. D. Southall (1983) 'Memory for words in prose and their location on the page', *Memory and Cognition*, 11, 429–34.

Luchins, A. S. (1942) 'Mechanisation in problem solving', *Psychological Monographs*, 54, No.6.

Luria, A. R. and F. I. Yudovich (1956) *Speech and the Development of Mental Processes in the Child* (London: Staples Press; new edn. 1971 Penguin).

Mackworth, N. H. (1950) 'Researches on the measurement of human performance', *Medical Research Council Special Report*, No. 268 (London: HMSO).

Marks, W. B., W. H. Dobelle and E. F. MacNichol (1964) 'Visual pigments of single primate cones', *Science*, 143, 1181–3.

Matlin, M. W.(1989) *Cognition*, 2nd edition (Fort Worth: Holt, Rinehart & Winston).

Maurer, D. and M. Barrera (1981) 'Infants' perceptions of natural and distorted arrangements of a distorted face', *Child Development*, 52, 196–202.

McClelland, J. L. and D. E. Rumelhart (1981) 'An interactive activation model of context effects in letter perception: Part I: An account of basic findings', *Psychological Review*, 88, 375–407.

McGeoch, J. A. and W. T. Macdonald (1931) 'Meaningful relations and retroactive inhibition', *American Journal of Psychology*, 43, 579–88.

McGinnies, E. (1949) 'Emotionality and perceptual defence', *Psychological Review*, 56, 244–51.

McKellar, P. (1972) *Imagination and Thinking: A Psychological Analysis* (New York: Cohen & West; 1st edn 1957).

McKoon, G., R. Ratcliffe and G. S. Dell (1986) 'A critical evaluation of the semantic-episodic distinction', *Journal of Experimental Psychology: Learning, Memory and Cognition*, 12, 295–306.

McNeill, D. (1966) 'The creation of language', in R. C. Oldfield and J. C. Marshall (eds), *Language* (Harmondsworth: Penguin).

Meacham, J. A. and J. Singer (1977) 'Incentive in prospective remembering', *Journal of Psychology*, 97, 191 7.

Miller, G. A. (1956) 'The magical number seven plus or minus two: Some limits on our capacity for processing information', *Psycholgical Review*, 63, 81–97.

Miller, G. A., E. Galanter and K. H. Pibram (1960) *Plans and the Structure of Behaviour* (New York: Holt, Rinehart & Winston).

Moray N. (1959) 'Attention in dichotic listening: Affective cues and the influence of instructions', *Quarterly Journal of Experimental Psychology*, 11, 56–60.

Morris, C. D., J. D. Bransford and J. J. Franks (1977) 'Levels of processing versus transfer appropriate processing', *Journal of Verbal Learning and Verbal Behaviour*, 16, 519–33.

Morris, P. E. (1978) 'Sense and nonsense in traditional mnemonics', in M. M. Gruneberg, P. E. Morris and R. N. Sykes (eds), *Practical Aspects of Memory* (London: Academic Press).

Moscovitch, M. and F. I. M. Craik (1976) 'Depth of processing, retrieval cues and uniqueness of encoding as factors in recall', *Journal of Verbal Learning and Verbal Behaviour*, 15, 477–58.

Naatanen, R. (1986) 'Neurophysiological basis of the echoic memory as suggested by event related potentials and magnetoencephalogram', in F. Klix and H. Hagendorf (eds), *Human Memory and Cognitive Capabilities* (Amsterdam: Elsevier).

Necker, L. A. (1832) 'Observations of some remarkable phenomena, seen in Switzerland: and an optical phenomenon which occurs on viewing of a crystal or geometrical solid.' *Phil. Mag.* I, 329.

Neisser, U. (1967) *Cognitive Psychology* (New York: Appleton).

Neisser, U. (1976) *Cognition and Reality* (San Francisco: W. H. Freeman).

Neisser, U. (1981) 'John Dean's memory: a case study', *Cognition*, 9, 1–2.

Neisser, U. (1982) *Memory Observed* (San Francisco: W. H. Freeman).

Nelson, K. (1981) 'Structure and strategy in learning to talk', *Monographs of the Society for Research in Child Development*, 38, Nos 1 and 2.

Nelson, T. O. and S. K. Vining (1978) 'Effect of semantic versus structural processing on long term retention', *Journal of Experimental Psychology: Human Learning and Memory*, 4, 198–209.

Newell, A. and H. A. Simon (1972) *Human Problem Solving* (Englewood Cliffs, N.J.: Prentice Hall).

Newson, J. (1974) 'Towards a theory of infant understanding', *Bulletin of the British Psychological Society*, 27, 251–7.

Nisbett, R. E. and T. D. Wilson (1977) 'Telling more than we can know: Verbal reports on mental processes', *Psychological Review*, 84, 231–59.

Norman, D. A. (1968) 'Towards a theory of memory and attention', *Psychological Review*, 75, 522–36.

Norman, D. A. (1969) 'Memory while shadowing', *Quarterly Journal of Experimental Psychology*, 21, 85–93.

Norman, D. A. (1976) *Memory and Attention: An Introduction to Human Information Processing*, 2nd edn (New York: Wiley).

Paivio, A. (1968) 'A factor-analytic study of word attributes and verbal learning', *Journal of Verbal Learning and Verbal Behaviour*, 7, 41–9.

Palmere, M., S. L. Benton, J. A. Glover and R. Ronning (1983) 'Elaboration and the recall of main ideas in prose', *Journal of Educational Psychology*, 75, 898–907.

Patten, B. M. (1972) 'The ancient art of memory', CMD, 39, 547–54.

Pavlov, I. P. (1927) *Conditioned Reflexes* (Oxford: Oxford University Press).

Peterson, L. R. and M. Peterson (1959) 'Short term retention of individual verbal items', *Journal of Experimental Psychology*, 58, 193–8.

Pettigrew, T. F., D. A. Allport and E. O. Barnett (1958) 'Binocular resolution and perception of race in South Africa', *British Journal of Psychology*, 49, 265–78.

Piaget, J. (1968) *Six Psychological Studies* (London: University of London Press).

Pillemer, D. B. (1984) 'Flashbulb memories of the assassination attempt on President Reagan', *Cognition*, 16, 63–80.

Pillemer, D. B., E. D. Rhinehart and S. H. White (1986) 'Memories of life transitions: The first year in college', *Human Learning*, 5, 109–23.

Pinker, S. (1984) 'Visual cognition: An introduction', *Cognition*, 18, 1–63.

Plato, *Republic*, Book X trans. Lindsay, A. D. (1935) (London: Dent Everyman's Library).

Pomerantz, J. R. (1981) 'Perceptual organisation in information processing', in M. Kubovy and J. R. Pomerantz (eds), *Perceptual Organisation* (Hillsdale, N.J.: Lawrence Erlbaum).

Postman, L., J. S. Bruner and E. McGinnies (1948) 'Personal values as selective factors in perception', *Journal of Abnormal and Social Psychology*, 43, 142–54.

Quinlan, P. T. and G. W. Humphreys (1987) 'Visual search for targets defined by combinations of color, shape and size: An examination of the task constraints on feature and conjunction searches', *Perception and Psychophysics*, 41, 455–72.

Ratcliffe, R. and G. McKoon (1978) 'Priming in item recognition: Evidence for the propositional structure of sentences', *Journal of Verbal Learning and Verbal Behaviour*, 17, 403–17.

Reason, S. J. (1984) 'Absent-mindednss and cognitive control', in J. E. Harris and P. E. Morris (eds), *Everyday Memory, Actions and Absent-mindedness* (London: Academic Press).

Riesen, A. H. (1950) 'Arrested vision', *Scientific American*, July 1950.

Rogers, T. B., N. A. Kuiper and W. S. Kirker (1977) 'Self-reference and the encoding of personal information', *Journal of Personality and Social Psychology*, 35, 677–88.

Rubin, D. C., E. Groth and D. J. Goldsmith (1984) 'Olfactory cuing of autobiographical memory', *American Journal of Psychology*, 97, 493–507.

Rubin, D. C. and M. Kozin (1984) 'Vivid memories', *Cognition*, 16, 81–95.

Rubin, D. C. and M. J. Olson (1980) 'Recall of semantic domains', *Memory and Cognition*, 8, 354–66.

Rubin, E. (1915) 'Synsoplevede Figurer', trans. D. C. Beardsley and M. Westheimer in *Readings in Perception* (Princeton: University Press).

Samuels, C. A. and R. Ewy (1985) 'Aesthetic perception of faces during infancy', *British Journal of Developmental Psychology*, 3, 221–8.

Scheerer, M. (1963) 'Problem solving', *Scientific American*, April 1963.

Schneider, W. and R. M. Shiffrin (1977) 'Controlled and automatic information processing: I: Detection search and attention', *Psychological Review*, 84, 1–66.

Schwartz, S. H. (1971) 'Modes of representation and problem solving: well-evolved is half solved', *Journal of Experimental Psychology*, 91, 347–50.

Segall, M. H., D. T. Campbell and M. J. Herskovitz (1966) *The Influence of Culture on Visual Perception* (New York: Bobbs-Merrill).

Selfridge, O. G. (1959) 'Pandemonium: A paradigm for learning', in *Symposium on the Mechanisation of Thought Processes* (London: HMSO).

Shaffer, L. H. (1975) 'Multiple attention in continuous verbal tasks' in P. M. Rabbitt and S. Dornic (eds), *Attention and Performance* (Vol. 5) (London: Academic Press).

Shapiro, P. N. and S. D. Penrod (1986) 'Meta-analysis of facial identification studies', *Psychological Bulletin*, 100, 139–56.

Shiffrin, R. M. and W. Schneider (1977) 'Controlled and automatic human information processing: II: Perceptual learning, automatic attending and a general theory', *Psychological Review*, 84, 127–90.

Shiffrin, R. M. and W. Schneider (1984) 'Automatic and controlled processing revisited', *Psychological Review*, 91, 269–76.

Sinclair-de-Zwart, H. (1969) 'Developmental psycholinguistics' in *Studies in Cognitive Development* (Oxford: Oxford University Press).

Skinner, B. F. (1957) *Verbal Behaviour* (New York: Appleton Century Crofts).

Slobin, D. I. (1973) 'Cognitive prerequisites for the acquisition of grammar', in C. A. Ferguson and D. I. Slobin (eds), *Studies of Child Language Development*, (New York: Holt, Rinehart & Winston).

Slobin, D. I. (1982) 'Universal and particular in the acquisition of language', in E. Wanner and L. R. Gleitman (eds), *Language Acquisition: The State of the Art* (Cambridge: Cambridge University Press).

Smith, E. E., E. J. Shoben and Rips, L. J. (1974) 'Structure and process in semantic memory: A featural model for semantic decisions', *Psychological Review*, 81, 214–41.

Smith, S. M., H. O. Brown, J. E. P Toman and L. S. Goodman (1947) 'Lack of cerebral effects of D-turbocurarine', *Anaesthesiology*, 8, 1–14.

Smith, S. M., A. Glenberg and R. A. Bjork (1978) 'Environmental context and human memory', *Memory & Cognition*, 6, 342–53.

Solley, C. M. and G. Murphy (1960) *The Development of the Perceptual World* (New York: Basic Books).

Sperling, G. (1960) 'The information available in brief presentations', *Psycholgical Monographs*, 74, 1–29.

Spoehr, K. T. and S. W. Lehmkuhler (1982) *Visual Information Processing* (San Francisco: W. H. Freeman).

Stacey, B. and R. Pike (1970) 'Apparent size, apparent depth and the Müller-Lyer illusion', *Perception and Psychophysics*, 7, 125–8.

Stewart, V. M. (1974) 'Tests of the "carpentered world" hypothesis by race and environment in America and Zambia', *International Journal of Psychology*, 8, 83–94.

Storms, M.D. and R. E. Nisbett (1970) 'Insomnia and the attribution process', *Journal of Personality and Social Psychology*, 2, 319–28.

Stratton, G. M. (1897) 'Vision without inversion of the retinal image', *Psychological Review*, 4, 341–60 and 463–81.

Stroh, C. M. (1971) *Vigilance – The Problem of Sustained Attention* (Oxford: Pergamon).

Thompson, C. P. (1982) 'Memory for unique personal events: The room-mate study', *Memory and Cognition*, 10, 324–32.

Thompson, C. P. (1985) 'Memory for unique personal events: Effects of pleasantness', *Motivation and Emotion*, 9, 277–89.

Thompson, C. P., J. J Skowronski and D. J. Lee (1987) 'Reconstructing the Date of a Personal Event', Paper Presented at the Second International Conference on Practical Aspects of Memory, Swansea.

Thorndike, E. (1988) *Animal Intelligence* (London: Macmillan).

Tousignant, J. P., D. Hall and E. F. Loftus (1986) 'Discrepancy detection and vulnerability to misleading post-event information', *Memory and Cognition*, 14, 329–38.

Treisman, A. M. (1960) 'Contextual cues in dichotic listening', *Quarterly Journal of Experimental Psychology*, 12, 242–8.

Treisman, A. M. (1964a) 'Verbal cues, language and meaning in selective attention', *American Journal of Psychology*, 77, 206–19.

Treisman, A. M. (1964b) 'Monitoring and storage of irrelevant messages in selective attention', *Journal of Verbal Learning and Verbal Behaviour*, 3, 449–59.

Treisman A. M. (1986) 'Features and objects in visual processing', *Scientific American*, 255(5), 114B–125.

Treisman, A. M. and G. Geffen (1967) 'Selective attention: Perception or response?', *Quarterly Journal of Experimental Psychology*, 19, 1–18.

Treisman, A. M. and G. Gelade (1980) 'A feature integration theory of attention', *Cognitive Psychology*, 12, 96–136.

Treisman, A. M. and J. G. A. Riley (1969) 'Is selective attention selective perception or selective response? A further test', *Journal of Experimental Psychology*, 79, 27–34.

Treisman, A. M. and H. Schmidt (1985) 'Illusory conjunction in the perception of objects', *Cognitive Psychology*, 14, 107–41.

Treisman, A. M. and J. Souther (1985) 'Search asymmetry: a diagnostic for preattentive processing of separable features', *Journal of Experimental Psychology: General*, 114, 285–310.

Trevarthen, C. (1974) 'Conversations with a one-month old', *New Scientist*, 62, 230–55.

Tulving, E. (1962) 'Subjective organisation in the free-recall of "unrelated words"', *Psychological Review*, 69, 344–54.

Tulving, E. (1972) 'Episodic and semantic memory', in E. Tulving and W. Donaldson (eds), *Organisation of Memory* (London: Academic Press).

Tulving, E. (1983) *Elements of Episodic Memory* (New York: Oxford University Press).

Turnbull, C. (1961) *The Forest People: A Study of Pygmies of the Congo* (New York: Simon & Schuster).

Tyler, S. W., P. T. Hertel, M. C. McCallum and H. C. Ellis (1979) 'Cognitive effort and memory', *Journal of Experimental Psychology: Human Learning and Memory*, 5(b), 607–17.

Ullman, S. (1984) 'Visual routines', *Cognition*, 18, 97–159.

Underwood, G. (1974) 'Moray vs. the rest: The effects of extended shadowing practice', *Quarterly Journal of Experimental Psychology*, 26, 368–72.

van der Heijden, A. H. C. (1981) *Short Term Visual Information Forgetting* (London: Routledge & Kegan Paul).

Vernon, M. D. (1970) *Perception through Experience* (London: Methuen).

Von Wright, J. M., K. Anderson and U. Stenman (1975) 'Generalisation of conditioned GSR's in dichotic listening' in P. M. A. Rabbitt and S. Dornic (eds), *Attention and Performance* Vol. 5 (London: Academic Press).

Vygotsky, L. S. (1962) *Thought and Language* (Cambridge, Mass.: MIT Press).

Wade, N. J. and M. Swanston (1991) *Visual Perception* (London: Routledge).

Watson, J. B. (1913) 'Psychology as the behaviourist views it', *Psychological Review*, 20, 158–77.

Weisberg, R. W. and J. W. Alba (1981) 'An examination of the alleged role of "fixation" in the solution of several "insight" problems', *Journal of Experimental Psychology: General*, 110, 169–92.

Webber, S. M. and P. H. Marshall (1978) 'Bizarreness effects in imagery as a function of processing level and delay', *Journal of Mental Imagery*, 2, 291–300.

Wilkinson, R. T., H. C. Morlock and H. L. Williams (1966) 'Evoked cortical response during vigilance', *Psychonomic Science*, 4, 221–2.

Witkin, H. A. (1949) 'The nature and importance of individual differences in perception', *Journal of Personality*, 18, 145–70.

Wollen, K. A., A. Weber and D. H. Lowry (1972) 'Bizarreness versus interaction of mental images as determinants of learning', *Cognitive Psychology*, 2, 518–23.

Wood F., B. Taylor, R. Penny and D. Stump (1980) 'Regional cerebral bloodflow response to recognition memory versus semantic classification tasks', *Brain and Language*, 9, 113–22.

Worthington, A. (1969) 'Paired comparison scaling of brightness judgements: A method for the measurement of perceptual defence', *British Journal of Psychology*, 60 (3), 363–8.

Yerkes R. M. and J. D. Dodson (1908) 'The relation of strength of stimulus to rapidity of habit formation', *Journal of Comparative Neurology and Psychology*, 18, 459–82.

Index

192